# WEAPON

# PANZERFAUST AND PANZERSCHRECK

## GORDON L. ROTTMAN

Series Editor Martin Pegler

First published in Great Britain in 2014 by Osprey Publishing,
PO Box 883, Oxford, OX1 9PL, UK
PO Box 3985, New York, NY 10185-3985, USA
E-mail: info@ospreypublishing.com

Osprey Publishing is part of the Osprey Group

A CIP catalogue record for this book is available from the British
Library

Print ISBN: 978 1 78200 788 3
PDF ebook ISBN: 1 78200 789 0
ePub ebook ISBN: 1 78200 790 6

Index by Mark Swift
Typeset in Sabon and Univers
Battlescenes by Johnny Shumate
Cutaways by Alan Gilliland
Originated by PDQ Media, Bungay, UK
Printed in China through Worldprint Ltd

15 16 17 18   10 9 8 7 6 5 4 3 2

Osprey Publishing is supporting the Woodland Trust, the UK's
leading woodland conservation charity, by funding the dedication
of trees.

www.ospreypublishing.com

## Acknowledgements

The author is indebted to Tom Laemlein of Armor Plate Press,
Nik Cornish at www.stavka.org.uk and Ted Nevill of Cody
Images for the use of photographs, and to Edward Rudnicki for
sharing reference materials. Thanks, too, to Mike Lebens of the
National Museum of the Pacific War, Fredericksburg, Texas.

## Author's note

The armour penetration ability information for various
projectiles quoted in this work is taken from official documents.
The penetration is based on the projectile striking the armour at
zero degrees under ideal conditions. The reality is that projectiles
seldom strike at zero degrees, either because of the angle of
impact and/or the slope of the armour. For these reasons they
often penetrate less deeply than official documents claim.

## Editor's note

In this work the abbreviation 'Pzf' is employed in conjunction
with the model designator – Pzf 30, 60, 100 and 150 – to
designate *Panzerfaust* variants, but this abbreviation was very
little used in World War II. It has been used in the post-war
period for more recent weapons sharing the name *Panzerfaust*.
Because the Germans used the metric system during World War
II, all measurements in this book are in metric. For ease of
comparison please refer to the following conversion table:

1km = 0.62 miles
1m = 1.09yd / 3.28ft
1cm = 0.39in
1mm = 0.04in
1kg = 2.20lb / 35.27oz

Front cover images are (top) © Royal Armouries PR.1788 and
(bottom) courtesy of Tom Laemlein/Armor Plate Press.
Title page: A two-man *Panzerschreck* team in training, Germany,
June 1944. (Cody Images)

# CONTENTS

# INTRODUCTION

By the end of 1940 the tank had undeniably proved to be a dominant weapon on European and North African battlefields. Most of the period's anti-tank weapons were woefully inadequate and, by 1942, mostly obsolete. Tank armour improved though better heat treating methods, increased use of sloping armour, and simply thicker armour. Most countries employed light anti-tank guns in the 37mm-calibre range and the infantry lugged anti-tank rifles heavier than their machine guns. Some used marginally effective anti-tank hand and rifle grenades, these being many countries' first weapons to use the shaped charge to penetrate armour. Molotov cocktails, satchel charges thrown onto engine decks and landmines shoved into treads were last-resort measures and virtual suicide weapons, contributing little to a viable anti-tank defence.

Despite the dramatic successes of the *Blitzkrieg* tactics in the first part of World War II, experience of Nazi Germany's infantry soldiers with respect to the threat posed by enemy armour was much the same as that of the other combatants. Conventional anti-tank guns were heavy and expensive; Germany's anti-tank rifles were obsolete, and the rifle grenades employed by the Wehrmacht, Germany's armed forces, could not deliver a large enough shaped charge – because of excessive recoil – to be effective against medium and heavy tanks. When German troops confronted the Russian T-34 tank in June 1941, it did not take long to realize that most current anti-tank weapons were obsolescent at best. The T-34's comparatively thick and well-sloped armour made it a formidable opponent. What was desperately needed was an anti-tank weapon that allowed the individual soldier to kill a tank. The initial attempt to find a solution – the hand-delivered shaped charge – would prove to be a weapon of desperation; it could disable a tank, but being hand-delivered represented a sure way of receiving the Iron Cross ... posthumously. A better means of delivery allowing some degree of stand-off – that is, not having to come into physical contact with the tank – was necessary.

Two soldiers of Panzergrenadier-Division *Großdeutschland*, the Heer's premier combat unit during World War II, each carrying a Pzf 30 (groß). In the background is their camouflaged SdKfz 251/1 half-tracked armoured personnel carrier. It was common for two or three *Panzerfäuste* to be carried in half-tracks. (Tom Laemlein/Armor Plate Press)

Long range was desired for most anti-tank weapons, to allow engagement with as much distance as possible between the weapon and the enemy tank – terrain permitting – before the enemy tank and its accompanying infantry closed to within optimal ranges. Not all such weapons needed long range, though. Infantrymen in Germany's rifle companies, holding or taking ground, needed a different kind of anti-tank weapon. They needed to be able to effectively engage tanks that were about to overrun their positions at ranges of 200m or less, and usually at even shorter ranges. The infantryman's ideal anti-tank weapon also had to be light and compact enough to carry easily over rough terrain or through rubble or dense vegetation, and allow its carriers to keep up with riflemen.

While much is made of tanks wreaking havoc among infantry – and that can be devastating – the intermixing of tanks and enemy foot-soldiers can also be a dangerous situation for tankers, especially if the tanks have been separated from their accompanying infantry by mortars and machine guns. Infantrymen like to defend on difficult ground. This could be within forests or other dense vegetation, broken ground with gullies, rock outcroppings, hillocks, etc.; among buildings or rubble; or amid unfavourable ground conditions such as bogs, marshes, and mud. In such conditions, tankers have to watch for anti-tank obstacles, mines, rubble, tree stumps, and so on. These environments provide infantrymen with cover and concealment, plus they tend to dig holes in the ground. On such terrain, infantrymen can manoeuvre in concealment to position themselves

to engage tanks from the ideal location in the flanks and rear. In effect, they can stalk tanks. Light, compact weapons were necessary for that. Reliability, simplicity of operation, range, accuracy, and lethality were of course necessary and efforts to improve these capabilities were constant.

In the event, two German weapons – the *Panzerfaust* and the *Panzerschreck* – would emerge in quick succession. Both were man-portable, shoulder-fired, recoilless infantry anti-tank weapons. Owing much to the American bazooka, the crew-served *Panzerschreck* would essentially replace battalion and regimental-level anti-tank weapons and would be used *en masse* to compensate for its moderate range and accuracy. Heavier, more awkward to handle and offering less armour penetration, it was somewhat longer-ranged and a little more accurate than the *Panzerfaust*. By the war's end, however, improved *Panzerfäuste* would offer a range approaching that of the *Panzerschreck* – indeed, the developmental Pzf 250 was intended to replace the *Panzerschreck*. Conversely, the *Panzerfaust* was unlike any previous weapon; an individual weapon with no dedicated crew, it was intended to be issued and used at rifle-company level and below. It was no *Wunderwaffe* (wonder weapon), but because it was so rapidly produced, easy to operate and employed in large numbers – and effective – it would have a lasting impact on the battlefield, both during and after World War II.

Belgium, winter 1944/45: US troops of the 1st Infantry Division examine three abandoned Pzf 60s along with some damaged Kar 98k carbines. Owing to the presence of the damaged weapons, these *Panzerfäuste* may well have been misfires and dangerous to handle. (Tom Laemlein/Armor Plate Press)

**OPPOSITE**
A Finnish soldier carries a *Panzerschreck*, a weapon the Finns called the *88mm:n raketinheitin mallia B54* ('88mm of the rocket launcher model B54'). It appears that the sight-port glass piece is missing. The replacement glass storage bracket is above the hand guard. Finnish *Panzerschreck* crews were often armed with Suomi m/31 submachine guns, even though such weapons were heavier than the usual Mosin-Nagant rifle carried by the infantry. (Tom Laemlein/Armor Plate Press)

# DEVELOPMENT
## A melding of technologies

### TECHNICAL ORIGINS

The *Panzerfaust* was a recoilless projector, while the *Panzerschreck* was a recoilless rocket launcher. Both of these designs would draw upon developing technologies, combining them in new ways to transform the fortunes of the infantryman faced with enemy armour on the battlefield.

### The shaped charge

An innovative explosive technique revolutionized the design of armour-defeating munitions. The shaped charge or hollow charge – known in the United States as a high-explosive anti-tank (HEAT) warhead – would be widely used during World War II as a means of penetrating armour and other hardened targets. Shaped charges were used in hand and rifle grenades, hand-emplaced demolition charges, anti-tank and tank guns, anti-tank rocket launchers, recoilless rifles, light field artillery, anti-aircraft guns (against ground targets) and aerial bombs. One of the main benefits of the shaped-charge projectile is that it does not rely on velocity or kinetic energy mass to penetrate armour. A shaped-charge round will achieve the same penetration at 500m range as it will at 50m or if simply hand-emplaced against it. It makes no difference if the projectile is hand-thrown or fired from a high-velocity gun; the penetration will be the same, if the projectiles are of the same size and design.

The projectile is comparatively light and inexpensive, as no hardened-steel penetrator is required. Armour two to three times the diameter of the cone can be penetrated. Upon impact the projectile is detonated by a base-detonating fuse (some used less effective point-detonating fuses), and the cone's metal lining is formed into a molten 'hot solid slug' that punches through armour plate at approximately 10,000m/sec. This process is

usually described as the liner being vaporized into a plasma jet that instantly burns through armour. This is not entirely correct. This 'slug' of molten metal carries with it fragments from both the projectile and the armour itself. The hot slug and fragments will ignite ammunition and fuel and kill anyone in their path. Eventually the slug breaks up into smaller particles and little further penetration occurs. The hole created is surprisingly small in diameter and the outer entry hole is larger in diameter than the interior exit hole.

Besides penetrating armour, shaped charges penetrate any hard surface such as concrete, masonry, timber or sandbags. Shaped charges also create secondary fragmentation that will injure personnel outside the target, although this is not excessive. Fin-stabilized shaped charges achieve far more effective penetration than spin-stabilized projectiles. Fin-stabilized projectiles do not rotate, or they rotate at a very low rate. The high rate of spin imparted on spin-stabilized projectiles (achieved by rifling) dissipates up to three-quarters of the penetrating effect through centrifugal force. This is why rocket-propelled shaped charges can use low-cost and lighter-weight smoothbore tubes. What stabilizes such projectiles are fins.

Shaped-charge warheads can be defeated, or their effects greatly reduced, by placing heavy wire mesh or thin steel plates a short distance from the armour plate. This causes the shaped charge to break up or to detonate short of the target and dissipates the effects of the plasma jet, resulting in little or no penetration.

Self-conscious troops of the US 36th Infantry Division in Southern France demonstrate the differences between the 8.8cm RPzB 54 and the 2.36in M1A1 bazooka – two weapons that would employ shaped-charge warheads to deadly effect during World War II. Note the kneeling grenadier to the far right with an M1 Garand rifle fitted with an M7 grenade launcher and an M9A1 anti-tank grenade. (Tom Laemlein/ Armor Plate Press)

## The origins of the shaped charge

Shaped-charge munitions rely on a principle known as the 'Munroe effect', named after Charles E. Munroe, a professor at the US Naval Academy when he first discovered it in 1888. Munroe did not perfect the weapon as an armour-penetrating charge; he simply demonstrated its effect. The principle employed an explosive charge with a cone-shaped cavity. The cavity placed against the target focused the blast on a narrow point and could cut a hole through metal or concrete.

During World War I, a German, Egon Neumann, improved the concept by lining the cavity with thin metal and detonating the charge, not directly against the target's surface, but a short distance from it – two to three times the diameter of the charge – to further focus the blast. He failed to perfect it for military use, however. Between 1935 and 1938, a Swiss chemical engineer and former Swiss Army machine-gunner, Henri J. Mohaupt, perfected the principle and demonstrated its use in demolition charges. In late 1940 he came to the United States and was involved in the development of the bazooka and other applications of the shaped-charge principle. A British ordnance engineer (name unknown), seeing the demonstrations, surmised the concept and designed the first grenade with a shaped-charge warhead, the No. 68 anti-tank rifle grenade.

It was the Germans, however, who first used the shaped charge in combat, which they referred to as the hollow charge (*Hohlladung*, or *H-Ladung*). A valuable contributor to the development of the shaped charge in Germany was Dr Franz R. Thomanek at the Luftwaffe's Luftfahrtforschungsanstalt (Aeronautical Research Institute) at Braunschweig, and later of the Luftwaffe's Ballistic Institute in Berlin. Thomanek is credited for developing the concept of the shaped-charge lined cavity in 1938–39. His early testing led to the discovery that a cone-liner more than doubled penetration, but it has never been resolved whether it was Mohaupt or Thomanek who discovered the concept first. The gun turrets of the Belgian fortress of Eben Emael were destroyed by glider-borne airborne troops using shaped-charge demolitions on 10 May 1940. It was not long before shaped-charge projectiles were developed for all sorts of weapons.

For many countries, the first use of the shaped-charge principle was in anti-tank rifle grenades. The United States developed the M9 anti-tank rifle grenade and the M10 grenade warhead based on Mohaupt's patent. The problem with the latter was how to deliver it. The M10 was too heavy to be launched from rifles (even a rocket-assisted version was tested on rifles) and the .50-calibre M2 machine gun with a launcher proved to be less than ideal. It was finally fitted to a small rocket motor and became the warhead for the 2.36in bazooka anti-tank rocket launcher. (Artwork by Hugh Johnson © Osprey Publishing)

## The rocket projector

Until the end of 1941, rockets had always been designed to lift heavier and larger warheads – artillery-level weapons. None was man-portable, much less hand-held. The Germans had been working on rocket projectors since 1931, and the Wehrmacht established *Nebelwerfer* units armed with multiple-tube rocket launchers after the French campaign in time for the invasion of the Soviet Union. Rockets were notoriously inaccurate, but they offered key advantages over conventional artillery pieces. Unlike a conventional gun, which was typically extremely heavy and had to withstand tremendous recoil, the rocket launcher could propel a heavy projectile at a high velocity from a comparatively light weapon; since the blast was directed out of the launcher's breech, it countered the effects of recoil, allowing for a light-weight mounting. Additionally, since the rocket projectile did not have to resist the direct detonation of the propellant to propel it, it could be of lighter construction. This allowed the thin-walled rocket projectile to carry a much larger explosive charge than a thick-walled cast-iron projectile weighing the same could carry.

## The recoilless projector

Another propelling system similar to, and sometimes confused with, the rocket is the recoilless projector – what the Germans initially called the *Düsenkanone* (nozzle cannon). A rocket motor burns for a comparatively

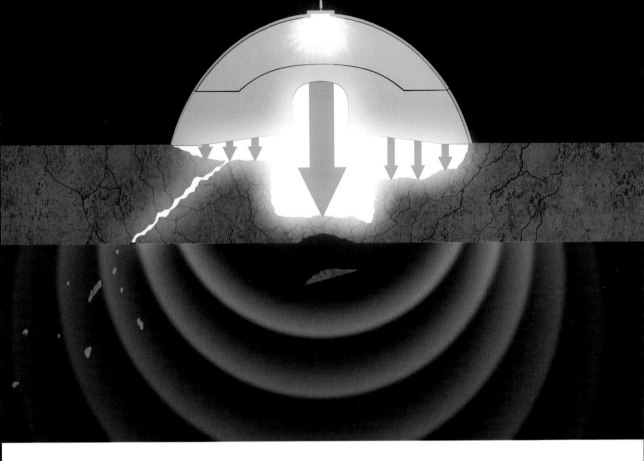

long time – fractions of a second or longer – rather than an instantaneous detonation like an artillery propellant charge. The propellant is preferably completely burned within the tube, but it can also continue to burn briefly after leaving the launch tube. A recoilless projector's propellant does not have a 'prolonged' burn, however. The propellant charge detonates along the lines of the propellant in a rifle's enclosed metallic cartridge case. This of course generated recoil. In a recoilless projector, half of the propellant's thrust propels the projectile out of the tube or barrel, while the other half is vented out of the breech to counter the recoil.

German development of such weapons began in the early 1930s and eventually resulted in a series of light recoilless artillery pieces – *leicht Geschützen* (light guns). These were basically substitutes for field artillery, and were developed for use by airborne and mountain troops as they were lighter and more portable. Some models had a secondary anti-tank capability.

A 2cm S-18-100 anti-tank rifle, as used in German service. A daunting 1,760mm long and weighing 45kg without its five- or ten-round magazine, the S-18-100 suffered from tremendous recoil. Unless employed in static positions, such weapons offered little to foot-soldiers confronted with enemy armour at close quarters. (Cody Images)

# TOWARDS THE *PANZERFAUST*

## The Panzerwurfgranate 41

In October 1941 the requirement for a new weapon, the Panzerwurfgranate 41 ('[anti]-armour thrown grenade 1941'), stated it was to weigh no more than 0.5kg to allow a throwing range of 10–15m. Two firms began work, Richard Rinker GmbH in Neubrandenburg and Westfalische Anhaltische Sprengstoff Aktiengesellschaft (WASAG, or 'Westfalian Anhalt Explosives Stock Company') in Wittenberg. Both firms presented prototypes, which were field-tested on the Eastern Front in early 1942. Each consisted of a pentolite-filled, base-detonating, impact-fused, shaped-charge warhead with a 100mm-diameter hemispherical nose cap, and a throwing handle containing fabric stabilizing ribbons. When thrown, the stabilizing ribbons streamed behind to ensure the grenade impacted on the target at the desired angle to achieve detonation and effective penetration.

Both firms' grenades experienced difficulties, with the stabilizers failing to deploy consistently and only 30–35mm of armour penetration being achieved. The short throwing range made it a dangerous weapon for the infantryman; he was exposed to close-range fire and since the grenades detonated on impact, he could be wounded or killed by its blast and fragmentation. If the weapon was inadvertently dropped after arming, it could detonate. Since a sufficiently large shaped-charge warhead could not be hand-thrown from a safe range, it was reasoned that perhaps it could be propelled to the target by some means. Rifle grenades could not launch a large enough shaped charge, while larger grenade projectors like the GrB 39 were as heavy as anti-tank rifles. A small hand-held rocket launcher or recoilless projector might be the answer.

Details are limited about *Panzerfaust* development and testing by Hugo Schneider Aktiengesellschaft (HASAG, or 'Hugo Schneider Stock Company'), headquartered in Leipzig. In 1932 SS-Sturmbannführer Paul Budin was assigned as general manager; in April 1945, as the Allies closed in on Leipzig, Budin blew up the HASAG offices and main buildings along with himself, his family and the firm's records. Besides in-house developmental testing by HASAG, extensive reliability and effectiveness testing was undertaken by the Heereswaffenamt (HWA, or 'Army Weapons Office'). This was the responsibility of its Waffenamt Prüfwesen 11

Portable, easy to operate and deadly at close ranges, the *Panzerfaust* would fill a very real battlefield need for German foot-soldiers confronted by enemy armour. Here, a *Feuerwerker* (artificer) – equivalent to an *Oberfeldwebel* (senior field sergeant) – demonstrates the kneeling underarm firing position for the Pzf 30 (groß). The Gothic 'F' sleeve insignia indicates his appointment as an ordnance NCO; one was assigned to each regiment. (Cody Images)

(Wa Prüf 11 – Abteilung für Sondergerät, or 'Weapons Proofing Office 11 – Branch for Special Equipment'), which was responsible for rockets and related equipment. HWA testing was carried out at the Versuchsstelle-West ('Experimentation Station') at Kummersdorf, south of Berlin. The HWA gave HASAG a great deal of latitude in regards to the *Panzerfaust*'s development and testing. After all, the firm had come up with the concept, and managed all aspects of its development from start to finish. While there were component subcontractors involved, HASAG handled end-product production, fixed problems and made improvements.

The first attempt at a handheld recoilless anti-tank projector was less than a success, however.

## The Faustpatrone 42

Dr Heinrich Langweiler headed HASAG's research department, supported by an eventual staff of ten qualified scientists and 250 technicians, assistants and workers. He would lead the effort to design and field a small one-man recoilless anti-tank weapon, and oversee its progressive development through all of the *Panzerfaust* models. HASAG's development of the FP 42 began in November 1942, with the rejection of the Panzerwurfgranate 41. Rather than attempting to hand-throw a sufficiently heavy shaped-charge grenade capable of defeating tanks, it was reasoned that a hand-fired anti-armour grenade could be used. The FP 42 consisted of a short 28mm-calibre launch-tube housing a propellant charge, a friction firing igniter and an over-calibre, shaped-charge warhead 80mm in diameter with a hemispherical nose cap. It was essentially a modified Panzerwurfgranate 41 with a finless tailboom and kleine Zündladung 34 ('small booster charge 1934') fitted. It was approximately 350mm long – warhead and launch tube – and weighed 1kg.

The FP 42 was operated by unscrewing the cap of the friction igniter under the short launcher tube (a modified Eihgr 39 fuse with the delay

element removed) and pulling the cord to ignite the black-powder propellant charge. This was not a rocket, but a handheld recoilless projector. Its maximum range was 70m, but effective range was only 20–30m. It was a one-shot weapon; once fired, the launcher tube was discarded. It saw only very limited field testing on the Eastern Front in early 1943.

The FP 42's short tube made it difficult to hold the weapon and keep the cone-shaped exhaust port clear of the firer's body, much less to aim it. It had to be held off to the side. The propellant was supposed to burn completely in the tube. However, burning propellant particles could be blown back on to the firer, especially his hand. This was even more of a problem in cold temperatures, which caused the propellant to burn more slowly. Gloves were essential. The FP 42 was not well received by the troops owing to its short range, awkward handling, difficult aiming and the danger posed by back blast. Nor was it easy to hit a static target, much less a moving one. In order to attack a tank with an FP 42, the user had to be within pistol or grenade range of a tank, both of which close-range weapons tank crews carried for close-in defence. If accompanying enemy infantry were present, the FP 42 definitely lacked the necessary stand-off range.

It was immediately obvious to Langweiler what improvements were necessary to field a workable weapon. A longer launcher tube, less than a metre long, would allow it to be held under the arm, with the tube clamped against the torso's side by the arm. Aiming could be accomplished by placing a folding sight on the top of the tube and aligning it with the top edge of the projectile to the desired impact point on the target. It was crude at best. A firing button would be located atop the tube behind the folding sight. The warhead was removable in order to load the detonator and primer, but the propelling charge would be fixed inside the tube. Like the FP 42, this new weapon was designed to be fired once and the launcher tube discarded. This was an entirely novel idea. Essentially, the launcher and warhead was a single round of ammunition issued complete, four to a box, with little preparation required. Simplicity of design and use were paramount. Even an inexperienced person, including inducted civilian Volkssturm personnel unfamiliar with any kind of weapons, could be taught its use in 15 minutes.

## THE *PANZERFAUST* DESCRIBED

Before discussing the different *Panzerfaust* models, a general description of the basic weapon is appropriate. They were all similar in design, but each new model offered refinements and improved capabilities.

### The projectile

The *Panzerfaust*'s over-calibre projectile, simply called the head (*Kopf*) consisted of a nose cap and the lower portion of the projectile body with an integral tail tube. It contained the *Pentol*-filled hollow charge behind the cone-shaped liner. A spring steel clip or lock was on the base of the body latched to a spring steel collar attached to the tailboom. This aligned the projectile so that the sight bead on its rim lined up with the folding rear sight. The tail tube contained the booster charge and primer. On the end of this was a wooden tail shaft with the four folding tailfins.

The Pzf 30 (groß), Pzf 60 and Pzf 100 used the basic 140mm over-calibre projectile (*Körper*) or grenade (*Granate*) – simply called the head (*Kopf*). It consisted of a blunt nose cap (*Kappe*) and the lower portion of the projectile body (*Geschoßkörper*) with a 44mm-diameter tail tube (*Geschoßzapfen*). It was made entirely of pressed sheet steel (*Stahlblech*). Inside the body was the thin sheet-steel insert (*Einlage*) – the liner for the shaped charge (*Hohlladung*). This was backed by 0.8kg of *Pentol*, a heavy explosive charge for a shaped-charge of this size. (For comparison, the American 2.36in (60mm) bazooka rocket carried a little under 8oz (0.22kg) with a 4.7in (120mm) penetration under ideal conditions and zero degrees impact.) Most models of *Panzerfaust* could penetrate 200mm.

A member of the Volkssturm training with the *Panzerfaust*, November 1944. (Cody Images)

The Pzf 30 (klein) had a 95mm-calibre warhead of a different shape and contained only 0.4g of *Pentol*. The tail shaft (*Leitwerkschaft*) was a two-piece wooden shaft to which were riveted four 100mm-long, rectangular, thin sheet-metal folding fins (*Flügel*). Some fins were triangular. There was a metal reinforcing cap on both ends. The fins wrapped around the shaft anticlockwise. Inside the tail tube was a cavity for the kleine Zündladung 34 over which the larger Faustpatrone primer (Faustpatronezünder FPZ 8001, 8002 or 8003, for Pzf 30, Pzf 60, and Pzf 60 and Pzf 100, respectively) were inserted before firing. A steel spring clip (*Blattfader*) or lock (*Sperre*) on the lower portion of the body clipped to a spring steel collar on the upper end of the tail shaft to align the projectile so the sight bead (*Korn*) (on the Pzf 60 and later) on its rim lined up with the rear sight. The complete projectile weighed 2.9kg. Overall length was 492mm.

## The tube

The launcher tube (*Rohr*) was simply an 809mm-long steel tube; the tube for the Pzf 30 (klein) was 33mm in diameter. Although some references claim the Pzf 60 had a 50mm-diameter tube and the Pzf 100 one of 60mm, from the Pzf 30 (groß) onwards the *Panzerfäuste* were all 44mm in diameter. A folding sight (*Visier*) was on top of the muzzle. Directly behind

**OPPOSITE**
A surviving Pzf 60 in the collection Britain's Royal Armouries.
(© Royal Armouries PR.1788)

15

this was the trigger lever (*Abzug* or *Klinke*). The sights and trigger mechanisms differed greatly between the Pzf 30 and the Pzf 60 and later models. The folded sight was held in place by a latch pin (*Vorstecker*) on the right side of the sight. Beneath the trigger was the safety bar (*Sicherung*). When the sight was raised, the weapon was armed to fire.

The non-removable black powder (*Schwarzpulver*) propellant charge contained in a cardboard tube with its small firing primer – a different primer from the larger one loaded into the projectile's tail tube – was fixed inside the tube below the trigger. It was not part of the projectile. The Pzf 100 had a second propellant charge fixed about a third of the tube's length from the breech. A waterproofed paper cap or cover (*Pappkappe* or *Deckel*) was fixed on the breech to prevent the entry of dust, dirt, mud, water and snow.

Their weight ranged from 3.2kg for the Pzf 30 (klein) up to 6.8kg for the Pzf 60 and Pzf 100. Designated by their optimal range in metres (30, 60, 100 and 150), they could reach double that range, but accuracy fell off quickly beyond the optimal range owing to the projectile's heavy weight causing a rapid drop in trajectory, air resistance on its broad cross-section and crosswind effects on the large finned projectile.

## *PANZERFAUST* VARIANTS

### The Panzerfaust 30 (klein) and Panzerfaust 30 (groß)

The first two *Panzerfaust* models were developed and fielded in parallel. The intent was to field a smaller model for use against light armour and a larger one for heavier tanks. While of the same basic design and operating in exactly the same way, the Pzf 30 (klein) and Pzf 30 (groß) were essentially two different weapons. Officially, the two weapons were designated the Panzerfaust 30 (klein) and simply Panzerfaust 30 (without 'groß'). In this study, 'Pzf 30 (klein)' and 'Pzf 30 (groß)' will be used where necessary to differentiate between the two. To the German soldier the small and large Pzf 30 models were simply called the *kleiner und spitz* ('smaller and pointed') and *größer und abgestumpft* ('larger and blunted' or 'truncated').

Initially known as the FP 1, the Pzf 30 (klein) had a 33mm-diameter tube with a small 95mm-diameter nipple-shaped warhead of a very different design from the larger style found on all subsequent *Panzerfäuste* variants. The Pzf 30 (klein)'s booster charge and primer were inserted in the tail tube that was not surrounded by explosives. The booster was held in a wooden sleeve not found in other models. It relied on detonating the warhead charge with the booster charge exploding against the bottom end of the warhead. This did not always cause a positive detonation.

The Pzf 30 (groß) used a 44mm-diameter tube and the blunt 140mm warhead that would become the signature profile of the *Panzerfaust*. The Pzf 30 (groß)'s booster charge and primer tube, being larger in diameter, was surrounded by explosives to ensure a more positive detonation. Its tailboom was also longer than that of the Pzf 30 (klein).

The only components common to both models were the flip-up sight, firing mechanism, kleine Zündladung 34 and FPZ 8001 primer. The projectiles, not just the warheads, were of entirely different design, though with some similarities. Common between the two models were the firing mechanism and sight, which were very different from those of later models. The firing mechanism consisted of a round tube about 180mm long welded to the top of the launcher tube. In the forward end was a thin square rod with the striker on the rear end. The forward end of the rod ran through a vertical red-painted trigger button protruding from the top forward end of the tube. A spring was coiled around this. When the sight was raised after pulling out the latch pin from its forward end, the spring pushed the rod's forward end out of the tube's end and it was cocked. The weapon could not be fired unless the sight was raised. On the rear end was a protruding sleeve with a small red-painted stud. The sleeve

An officer explains the features of the Pzf 30 (groß) projectile to troops recently issued the *Panzerfaust*. The tail shaft with the four folding fins could be removed, but this was not necessary when loading the booster charge and primer. The two men behind the projectile are each holding the Pzf 30 (klein) with a smaller-calibre barrel. (Nik Cornish at www.stavka.org.uk)

# THE *PANZERFAUST* EXPOSED

## Pzf 30 (klein)

1. Shaped-charge cavity (*Hohlladung*) and liner (*Einlage*)
2. *Pentol* high-explosive filler
3. Locking collar
4. Booster charge (kleine Zündladung 34)

5. Primer (Faustpatronezünder FPZ 8001)
6. Tail shaft with four folding tailfins (one shown)
7. Propellant charge
8. Firing pin and spring

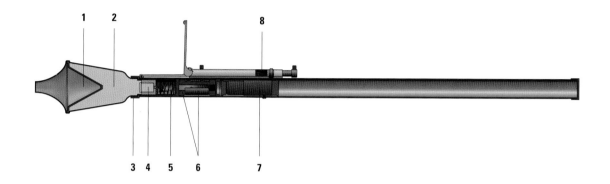

## Pzf 30 (groß)

1. Head (*Kopf*)
2. Latch pin (*Vorstecker*)
3. Folding sight (*Vizier*)
4. Trigger (*Abzug*)

5. Arming stud
6. Tube (*Rohr*)
7. Protective cap (*Pappekappe*)

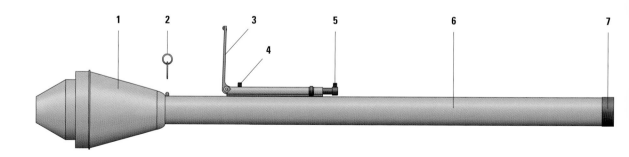

## Pzf 60

1. Nose cap (*Kappe*)
2. Lower projectile body (*Geschoßkörper*)
3. Folding sight

4. Trigger lever
5. Tube (*Rohr*)
6. Protective cap (*Pappekappe*)

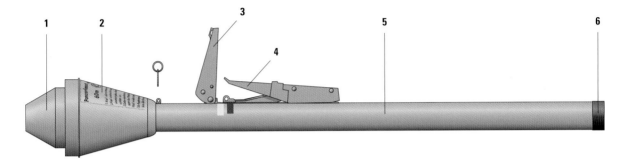

## Pzf 100

1. Shaped-charge cavity (*Hohlladung*) and liner (*Einlage*)
2. *Pentol* high-explosive filler
3. Locking collar
4. Booster charge (kleine Zündladung 34)

5. Primer (Faustpatronezünder FPZ 8003)
6. Tail shaft with four folding tailfins (one shown)
7. Front propellant charge
8. Rear propellant charge

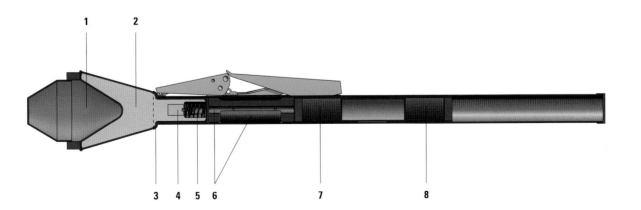

prevented the striker from hitting the primer. The stud was rotated to the left and the spring-loaded sleeve cleared the primer, making it ready to fire. When the trigger button was pressed the striker rod was released, the primer fired, and the propellant charge detonated.

The folding sight was extremely simple. It was hinged to the forward end of the firing mechanism tube and folded forward when not in use, being held in place by a latch pin. It was a narrow stamped sheet-metal strip with a rectangular hole with small projecting tabs on both sides. The 20m and 40m apertures were round, while the optimal 30m aperture was rectangular with indented sides. These were graduated for 20m, 30m and 40m. The firer aligned the necessary sight aperture with the top edge of the projectile's nose cap rim with the target. Chances of a hit over 30m were limited.

Langweiler's team began development of the Pzf 30 (klein) in December 1942 and the Pzf 30 (groß) in January 1943. The nipple shape of the Pzf 30 (klein)'s nose cap made it prone to glancing off sloped armour without detonating. The Pzf 30 (groß)'s nose cap and the entire warhead were enlarged; the blunt nose provided a 5cm-wide flat contact surface to ensure more positive detonation. Both models were successfully demonstrated at Kummersdorf in March 1943 and work on refinements continued.

In July 1943, 3,000 of both models were ordered for troop trials on the Eastern Front. They were issued in August and results were favourable; mass production commenced in October. Infantrymen liked their compactness and light weight, and the mobility such weapons gave them to move into advantageous firing positions. They were stunned that such a small, simple weapon could knock out a tank. The Pzf 30 (klein) was less used, but still useful – not that a soldier would turn down whatever was available.

The Pzf 30 (groß)'s 140mm warhead was found to be effective against T-34s, KV-1s, Shermans, Churchills and Matildas. It might not have always penetrated the frontal armour or gun mantlet, but it was effective with flank and rear shots. There were instances when the penetrating jet went out the opposite side of a turret after piercing the near side. Test firings had been conducted against 5cm and 10cm plates with a 5cm air gap between them. Factory proof testing was conducted by firing randomly selected *Panzerfäuste* at three 5.5cm armour plates with 6cm air spaces between each. No efforts were made to improve the penetration on later models. However, some testing was undertaken to find a better lining material for the shaped-charge cone. Tungsten was found to be more effective than the sheet steel in use. They apparently never discovered that copper was the most effective liner. Regardless, tungsten and copper were scarce materials. Further development concentrated on improving the range, accuracy and reliability of new *Panzerfaust* models. The firing systems on both models proved highly susceptible to moisture. The concept of small and large *Panzerfäuste* was dropped for subsequent models. Having mostly non-interchangeable components complicated manufacture, and the Pzf 30 (klein) did not offer much of a cost saving. Also, units were requesting mostly the Pzf 30 (groß) and not bothering with the Pzf 30 (klein).

## Panzerfaust models

| Model | Overall weight | Warhead weight | Overall length | Warhead calibre | Tube calibre | Propellant weight | Muzzle velocity |
|---|---|---|---|---|---|---|---|
| FP 42 | 1kg | unknown | 415mm | 80mm | 28mm | 30g | unknown |
| Pzf 30 (klein) | 3.2kg | 1.3kg | 985mm | 95mm | 33mm | 53.5g | 28m/sec |
| Pzf 30 (groß) | 5.22kg | 2.9kg | 1,045mm | 140mm | 44mm | 95g | 30m/sec |
| Pzf 60 | 6.8kg | 2.9kg | 1,045mm | 140mm | 44mm | 134g | 48m/sec |
| Pzf 100 | 6.8kg | 2.9kg | 1,045mm | 140mm | 44mm | 2×95g=190g | 62m/sec |
| Pzf 150 | 7kg | unknown | 1,045mm | 105mm | 44mm | 2×95g=190g | 82m/sec |
| *Splitterfaust* | unknown | unknown | unknown | 80mm | 44mm | 2×95g=190g | unknown |

The model number equates to the optimal effective range. All launcher tube lengths were 809mm except the Pzf 30 (klein), which had a 800mm tube. All models penetrated 200mm of armour at 0–30 degrees impact except the Pzf 30 (klein), with 140–160mm, and the Pzf 150, with 220mm. Note that some references appear to disagree with one another by providing slightly different characteristics.

## The Panzerfaust 60

The development of an improved high-power (*hochlauf*) *Panzerfaust* began in mid-1943 and was completed in early 1944. A larger propellant charge increased the velocity by about one-third and doubled the effective range. The 44mm-diameter launcher tube was made thicker to withstand the heavier propellant and rough field handling. The projectile included a number of refinements to make it stronger and more weatherproof and reliable. The major improvement was the firing mechanism. It was simpler to operate and more robust, but easier to produce.

The sight, too, was very different. A bead sight was added to the projectile's rim and a locking system provided that forced the projectile to be inserted where it would align the bead sight with the rear folding sight. The channel-shaped sight was held in the down position by a latch pin inserted from its right side at its top (forward) end. Folded, it served to lock the firing mechanism. When the pin was pulled and the sight raised, it freed the safety slide under the trigger lever. The slide was pulled forward to unlock the trigger. It could be slid back as a safety. With the slide forward, the bead sight was aligned with one of the three range apertures: 30m, 60m and 80m. Firing at anything beyond 60m meant a 50–70 per cent hit probability, less if the target was moving. Pressing downward on the front end of the trigger lever released a spring-steel snap-strip with a firing pin on its rear end. This was held in the up position by a notch on the inside rear of the trigger lever. When released, it snapped down, ignited the small primer, and the propellant charge detonated.

A US ordnance lieutenant examines the warhead of a Pzf 60. The retaining pin on the top of the sight has been removed and the sight raised. This armed the weapon. The pin would not be pulled until after the booster charge and primer were loaded into the tail tube. The red warning marking can be clearly seen on the barrel. The Pzf 100 appeared identical. (Tom Laemlein/Armor Plate Press)

The sight and firing mechanism appeared as two levers atop the launcher tube's forward end. With slight improvements the same sight and trigger were used on all subsequent models. This style of sight and trigger makes it easy to differentiate the later models from the Pzf 30 (groß).

With the massive production of the Pzf 60, large numbers became available on all fronts. It was not long before they were a fully accepted and commonly seen weapon. Still, the quest for extended range, improved accuracy, and greater reliability continued.

## The Panzerfaust 100

Development of the Pzf 100 began in the late summer of 1944 and was completed that September. It was essentially a Pzf 60 with a second 95g propellant change fixed about 15cm aft of the first charge, directly behind the projectile's tail assembly. When the weapon was fired, the first charge's detonation caused the instantaneous sympathetic detonation of the second. The air gap between the two charges eliminated the need for a heavier, reinforced launcher tube, which would have been necessary if the two had formed a single charge. This ingenious feature increased the velocity by 10m/sec without overly increasing the internal gas pressure.

The only other significant difference between the Pzf 100 and its precursors was the sight's range aperture settings: 50m, 100m and 150m. As with the Pzf 60, the longer range was only marginally effective. The only other noticeable refinement was that the sight holes were edged with yellowish-green luminous paint to improve night firing.

It is virtually impossible to differentiate the Pzf 60 from the Pzf 100 in photographs. The improved range and velocity, which increased accuracy, required no major changes or a noticeable increase in weight. A departure from early *Panzerfäuste* was the new FPZ 8003 primer, which meant the new *Panzerfaust* could be shipped in an armed state. This eliminated the need for the primer and booster charge to be packed separately, and for the projectile to be removed, the primer and booster inserted, and the projectile reloaded in the tube. Two months into production, the HWA rescinded this method and required them to again be packed separately and loaded in the field. This was because troops who were trained on the Pzf 100 and were not used to having to load the primer and booster were failing to load older Pzf 30s and Pzf 60s, assuming that all new-production *Panzerfäuste* were pre-loaded like the Pzf 100. This resulted in the firing of dud rounds.

An *Unteroffizier* demonstrates the loading of the *Panzerfaust* to his company officers. The kleine Zündladung 34 and primer have been loaded into the tail tube. The tail shaft with the four folding fins remained in the barrel along with the black-powder propellant change. (Nik Cornish at www.stavka.org.uk)

Production of the Pzf 100 was approved in November 1944 and they were arriving at the front by Christmas. The change-over from Pzf 60 to Pzf 100 production required little time and effort. At one point there was a lag in black-powder production owing to increased Allied bombing of production facilities. The Pzf 100 was the last of the 'traditional' *Panzerfäuste*.

## The Panzerfaust 150

While there are benefits to a single-shot, throwaway anti-tank weapon – simplicity, low cost, rapid production, ease of use – there were advantages to reloadable weapons. Throwaway weapons meant the launcher tubes were discarded, although they were sometimes recovered and returned to factories. Complete weapons with launcher tube and warhead, no matter how compact, meant more shipping space because of the requirement for bulkier shipping boxes. A box with two reloadable *Panzerfäuste* and boxes for 20 projectiles required less shipping space and weight – as well as fewer crating and packing materials – than five boxes containing four throwaway *Panzerfäuste* each.

Many references state the Pzf 150 was a single-shot weapon, while others say it was reloadable. Other sources say it was not produced beyond prototype form. The confusion lies in that the first Pzf 150s were single-shot. Development began in late 1944 and was completed in January 1945. Production commenced in February and by May 100,000 had been turned out. However, other than some prototypes issued for field testing, presumably on the Eastern Front, the weapon was not issued to combat troops. There is one photograph depicting a soldier in the field with a Pzf 150, but this might be during trials at the Infanterieschule (Infantry School) at Döberitz.

Further improvements to the ignition system were to be made and it was redesigned to be reloadable. This included making the propellant charges integral to the projectile to give it a longer tailboom. Feed-stripes of five ignition caps were to be inserted into the new firing mechanism by pushing subsequent caps into position with the thumb. Two stripes were to be issued with each launcher. It is surmised that only ten rounds could be fired from the light tube before inspection and cleaning were necessary – black-powder propellant is extremely fouling. This development was to have been completed by late May 1945 and series production would have commenced in the early summer. The reloadable Pzf 150 might have received a new designation if it had been produced.

Some references say the launcher tube was about 40mm longer than the Pzf 100's tube, but it may actually have been the same length. Other than that possibility, the Pzf 100's and Pzf 150's tubes were the same, in order to include the second propellant charge. The longer range was achieved by employing a lighter, more streamlined projectile. The Pzf 150 did not have a pistol grip or cone-shaped back blast deflector as pictured on a mockup of unknown origin – which may in fact be a mockup of a Pzf 250. The sight was graduated at 50m, 100m, 150m and 200m. A small front sight was fixed on the forward edge of the projectile's body. It and the apertures were painted with luminous paint.

A Luftwaffe *Obergefreiter* sights a prototype Pzf 150. This was the initial non-reloadable type. A reloadable Pzf 150 was under development at the war's end. It had a completely redesigned 105mm warhead as opposed to the customary 140mm warhead. (US Army)

The major difference from earlier models was the warhead, which deviated from the traditional design. It was smaller in diameter, at 105mm, with a long conical fluted nose and a cylindrical body. It is believed that the Soviet post-war RPG-2 rocket-propelled grenade launcher's PG-2 projectile was influenced by the Pzf 150. The shaped-charge cavity was hemispherical with a booster charge in the base end, which improved penetration. The shallower cavity required the longer nose for stand-off. The explosive charge was 900g. The reduction in explosives was beneficial, since explosives production in Nazi Germany was falling off.

The shaped-charge projectiles were poor anti-personnel weapons as most of the blast was directed into the ground and the shattering body broke up into a small number of large fragments. To make the projectile a more potent anti-personnel weapon, a fragmentation sleeve (*Splitterring*, or 'splinter ring') was developed for the Pzf 150 that slipped over the body and was held on by a metal constriction band. It was similar to the *Splitterring* on the Stg 24 hand grenade, but was segmented into square-shaped fragments. A sight extension, graduated to 300m and intended to be fitted on the raised sight, was attached to the stowed sleeve. The *Panzerfaust* could be used in this way at a longer range, as it was better suited for area fire, like a mortar, rather than for point targets. It would have been effective against tank-riding infantry as a dual-purpose weapon. The *Splitterring* would probably have been issued with the anti-tank projectiles, possibly on the basis of one sleeve per three projectiles, as was common with stick grenades.

Another innovation was the addition of a delay pellet to the base-detonating primer. If the projectile did not strike the target or the ground within three seconds, the projectile self-destructed. This avoided duds (blinds) when misses struck snow or soft ground. It also allowed airbursts to be achieved over troops in the open, or in open-topped positions, with the *Splitterring*. In theory it could be fired at low-flying aircraft. Realistically, however, the odds of damaging an aircraft were slim.

The Pzf 150 was produced by the Metallwarenfabrik Döbeln, Saxony, a facility that was occupied by the Soviets on 6 May 1945. As far as is known, no Pzf 150s survived the war. They were probably destroyed in the factory and at depots.

## EXPERIMENTAL *PANZERFÄUSTE*

A number of specialized *Panzerfäuste* were studied in late 1944 and 1945. Few were actually fabricated or tested.

### The Panzerfaust 250

The Pzf 250 only reached the drawing board. It is not certain if even mockups were made. A departure from traditional *Panzerfäuste*, it was to be reloadable with the intent of replacing the heavier and bulkier *Panzerschreck*. The Pzf 250 would have required a heavier launcher tube and probably an improved sight. It would have had a pistol grip with an integral trigger. There may have been a blast-deflector on the breech. The projectile was based on that of the Pzf 150, but with a larger integral propellant charge. Its muzzle velocity was projected to be 120–150m/sec.

A 10.5cm *Panzerfaust* was intended to combat a rumoured Soviet super tank under development called the *Schtschuka* ('pike') – it never existed. Two very different designs were proposed by HASAG and Dynamit Nobel AG, capable of defeating 400mm of armour; these were, respectively, the *groß Panzerfaust* and the 10.5cm *Hecht* ('pike' – named after the supposed tank it was intended to counter). The proposed weapons were too heavy and bulky for practical man-carrying.

Variations of *Panzerfäuste* were considered for anti-infantry use. The *Splitterfaust* ('fragmentation fist'), aka *Sprengfaust* ('bounding fist'), proposed in April 1944, was basically a Pzf 60 with an entirely different warhead. It was flat-nosed with a nose-detonating fuse. The body was scored with fragmentation segments. Upon ground impact the nose charge detonated to throw the projectile into the air to detonate at 3–4m. The HWA rejected it, preferring an add-on fragmentation sleeve, which was eventually developed for the Pzf 150. Another proposed anti-infantry weapon was the *klein Rakete für Infanterie Bekämpfung* ('small rocket for infantry combat'). This used the tube of a Pzf 60, but was a 66cm-long rocket fitted with a 76mm warhead that was 245mm long and made of

## *Panzerfaust* nicknames

The name of the *Panzerfaust* (pl. *Panzerfäuste*) literally translates as 'armour fist', this name implying that it would punch and knock out a tank. The first *Panzerfaust* versions, the Pzf 30 (klein) and the Pzf 30 (groß) were originally known as the FP 1 and FP 2, but were quickly retagged *Panzerfaust* as a more daunting name. The Pzf 30 (klein) was the only model bestowed with an official nickname: it was called the *Gretchen* (diminutive for *Gretel*, or 'Little Margaret'), or *kleine Gretel*. A second model fielded at the same time, the Pzf 30 (groß), seldom actually had 'groß' appended to its designation, though. *Panzerfaust* models were designated after their optimal range in metres (30, 60, 100, 150); the Pzf 30, Pzf 60 and Pzf 100, the most widely used models, were simply called *die dreißig* ('the thirty'), *die sechzig* ('the sixty'), and *die hundert* ('the hundred').

The German soldier's nicknames for the weapon included *Bumskeule*, literally meaning 'burn club'; the *Panzerfaust* did indeed look like a burning club with the back-blast flame flashing from the breech. It was also known as *die Patrone* ('the cartridge') as it was issued in a single unit like a small-arms cartridge (projectile, propellant, ignition system and case in one unit). The term *Marschallstab* was also used, implying the soldier held great authority when armed with a *Panzerfaust*, the marshal's baton being a sign of high military office. A more frank nickname was *Ivan Mörder* ('Ivan murderer'). Yet another nickname was *Spritze* ('syringe') – the *Panzerfaust* could give a deadly 'injection' to a tank. *Volks-Pak* (PaK = *Panzer-Abwehr-Kanone*, or 'anti-armour gun') meant the 'people's anti-armour gun', the 'people' in this case being the last-ditch Volkssturm militia and the 'gun' being the *Panzerfaust*, a poor substitute for a real anti-tank gun. The compact weapon's usefulness was implied by calling it a *wenig Helfer* ('little helper'). A little-used term was *Panzerabwehrrohr* ('armour defence tube'). The Germans apparently did not use or made little use of the truncated term *Faust*, as it was commonly called by the Americans and Soviets. Western Allied soldiers sometimes called the *Panzerfaust* the 'German bazooka' or 'Kraut bazooka', but that term was more commonly reserved for the *Panzerschreck*. 'Panzerfaust' was the common Allied name.

It is sometimes reported that *Panzerfaust* means 'armoured gauntlet', an old form of body armour protecting the forearm and hand. In German, however, 'gauntlet' is *Stulpe, Stulpenhandschuh* or *Panzerhandschuh*. (The German effort to keep Hungary on its side resulted in *Unternehmen Eisenfaust*, Hitler's bid to take over the Hungarian government. While often called Operation *Panzerfaust*, it is more accurately translated as Operation *Iron Fist*.)

concrete mixed with scrap metal. It was deemed unnecessary and rejected in 1944. The *Schrappnellfaust* ('shrapnel fist') was proposed in 1945 and apparently a few were made for testing just before the war's end. It was designed to throw an 8kg shrapnel-filled warhead 400m. A time fuse detonated it with an airburst 2–3m above ground.

Early 1945 saw the development of the *verbesserte Panzerfaust* ('improved armour fist') with a 160mm warhead and a variable-range detonation capability. This late in the war, however, prototype construction could not be accomplished. Another 1945 development was a *Panzerfaust* fitted with the traditionally shaped warhead, but made of *Nipolit*. This was a mixture of TNT, RDX (known as *Hexogen* to the Germans) and PETN, and reclaimed, unstable smokeless artillery propellants developed by WASAG. Its manufacture required the use of just over one-third the nitric acid, which was in critically short supply, that was needed to make the same amount of TNT. *Nipolit*, black to very dark grey in colour, could be cast or lathed into solid shapes. It was waterproof and possessed high structural strength, and no metal outer casing was necessary other than the nose cap.

Three types of incendiary warheads were considered. The *Panzerbrandgranate* ('armour incendiary projectile') was to have a shaped-charge warhead with an incendiary projectile (magnesium) in its base. The shaped charge would punch a hole and the incendiary projectile would follow through to ignite ammunition and fuel. The *Brandfaust* ('incendiary fist') warhead was a standard shaped charge with 30 per cent aluminium and barium peroxide (an oxidizer) mixed in. This would greatly increase the flame effect inside the tank. Aluminium shortages prevented its adoption. The *Flammfaust* (flame fist) used an unspecified liquid, probably thickened oil similar to that used in flamethrowers.

A final type of proposed variant was the *Reizgasfaust* ('irritant gas fist') with a warhead filled with CN type B – outdoor-use tear gas. There was little interest. Germany made virtually no use of tear gas in combat.

## *PANZERFAUST* PRODUCTION

The massive Hugo Schneider Aktiengesellschaft (HASAG) firm headquartered in Leipzig-Schönefeld, south-west of Berlin, was the primary *Panzerfaust* producer, along with the Schneider plant (Hugo Schneider, Schlieben Werk) south of Berlin. HASAG operated at least 11 other plants throughout Germany and one in Poland. Some of these plants produced component parts, as did other small firms. Robert Thümmler Metallwarenfabrik in Döbeln in eastern Germany also produced *Panzerfäuste*, but in small numbers. Volkswagen-Werke in Fallersleben west of Berlin produced all *Panzerfaust* tubes for both firms. The manufacturer's marks (*Herstellungzeichen*) for these plants found on weapons and certain components were: HASAG Leipzig-Schönefeld (wa), HASAG Schlieben Werk (wk), and Robert Thümmler Metallwarenfabrik (bdn).

The March 1945 issue of *Signal* magazine displayed six photos of what appear to be adequately clothed German men and women assembling *Panzerfäuste* in a HASAG factory. The posed workers could have been

German administrative staff. It is known that large numbers of forced-labour workers (*Zwangsarbeiter*) were employed in all aspects of *Panzerfaust* production at all involved plants. Many of the labourers were from Eastern Europe, mainly Poland, and most were women, for whom the SS charged less than men. Germans were placed in supervisory positions. The labourers were housed at the Buchenwald, Sachsenhausen, Ravensbrück and Schlieben-Berga concentration camps, with numerous sub-camps near factories. Over 15,000 labourers were employed at the HASAG factories at any one time – not all were involved in *Panzerfaust* production. Appalling working conditions meant that life expectancy was two to three-and-a-half months. In April and May 1945, when the factories were evacuated, the surviving labourers were forced by their German captors to undertake death marches westwards.

References disagree on production start dates and fielding dates for the various models of *Panzerfaust*. Once production began for a particular model it was at least a month or two, sometimes longer, before fielding commenced. They did not appear on all fronts or even in all sectors at the same time. Usually, the first lots were shipped to critical Eastern Front sectors before appearing in France and Italy. Initial fielding was in small lots to ensure the bugs were worked out. Minor modifications were made on the production lines within a couple of months and before large-scale production commenced.

Mass production of the *Panzerfaust* commenced in October 1943. A target monthly production rate of 100,000 Pzf 30 (klein) and 200,000 Pzf 30 (groß) was set, but was not achieved until April 1944. It took that long to expand the production lines, which was hampered by frequent bombings of the plants. By the time the goal was achieved, replacement models were available. Both models remained in use to the war's end and small numbers were still being turned out even in early 1945.

The Pzf 60 was in full production by September 1944, made more urgent by Western Allies' recent break-out from Normandy and the Soviet thrust into Eastern Europe. Some 400,000 were to be produced a month, a target that was accomplished in October. By December, 1.5 million a month were being run off production lines. Pzf 60 production was rapidly stepped up as Pzf 30 production lines were converted over to Pzf 60. *Panzerfaust* production not only did not fall owing to the changeover, but actually increased. Prior to late 1944, most *Panzerfäuste* were sent to the Eastern Front, with only small numbers appearing in Italy and France. More were eventually funnelled to the Western Front.

The following figures may not be accurate owing to lost and incomplete records during the war's final months. Huge numbers of *Panzerfäuste* were produced, with most issued to the troops. Records state only 271,000 were stored in depots. The 'produced' numbers include those distributed to units and those held in reserve stocks at corps- and army-level field depots.

In 1943, 123,900 Pzf 30 (klein) were produced, followed by 1,418,300 in 1944 and 12,000 in the first three months of 1945, for a total of 1,554,200. Only combined figures for the Pzf 30 (groß), Pzf 60 and Pzf 100 are available: 227,800 in 1943, 4,120,500 in 1944 and 2,251,800 in the first quarter of 1945, to total 6,600,100. Although 100,000 Pzf 150 were produced, these were not issued to units. Total *Panzerfaust* production was 8,254,300. Approximately one in eight *Panzerfäuste* were rejected by inspectors during the production process; these rejections were either corrected, or disassembled with their components returned to the production lines. It is likely that at least 800,000 (roughly 10 per cent) were recalled to factories owing to defects. Thousands more were returned by units due to defects.

Even so, while the Wehrmacht periodically experienced ammunition shortages, it seems there was always an abundance of *Panzerfäuste*. Photographs depict squads with almost as many *Panzerfäuste* as grenades. Realistically, a few hundred thousand *Panzerfäuste* were probably lost in action, being destroyed during transport by air attack and artillery, accidents, misfires, duds, abandoned during retreats, etc. Approximately 5–6 per cent (about 450,000) of the total number produced were misfires (*Zündversager*, or 'failed to fire') or duds (*Blinde*, or 'failed to detonate'). In theory, fired launcher tubes were to be recovered and shipped to factories. This was seldom done as troops in action did not bother to retain tubes and, with the Wehrmacht in retreat, this was not a priority.

## TOWARDS THE *PANZERSCHRECK*

The 8.8cm RPzB – *Raketenpanzerbüchse* (pl. *Raketenpanzerbüchsen*), or 'rocket [anti-]armour weapon' – better known as the *Panzerschreck* or *Ofenrohr*, was developed immediately after the first demonstrations of the *Panzerfaust* in early 1943. The *Panzerschreck* owed its rapid development to two distinct weapons systems, one German and the other American.

# The Raketenwerfer 43

One aspect contributing to the *Panzerschreck*'s development was the existence of the 8.8cm RPzgr 4312 round for the 8.8cm Raketenwerfer 43 ('rocket projector 43'). This small anti-tank rocket projector was mounted on a two-wheeled carriage and known as the *R-Werfer* or *Püppchen* ('Dolly'). Issued from September 1942, the *R-Werfer* looked like a miniature artillery piece with a small shield, two steel wheels with rubber treads, a single trail and a simple iron sight. Developed by WASAG by designer Dr Erich von Holt, it was intended to replace the rifle company's anti-tank rifles. 3,000 were built (some sources say 1,000), but it was expensive. Development began before the American bazooka was encountered, which spawned the development of the *Panzerschreck* and therefore led to the *R-Werfer*'s obsolescence.

Aiming was accomplished by hand traversing and elevating the barrel via a pair of handgrips beside the sliding breech block. The wheels could be removed to rest on a pair of short skids to lower its profile, or replaced by short snow skis. It was breech-loading and fired with a closed breech, causing it to generate recoil, but had no recoil-absorption system. The light carriage absorbed the recoil, transferring it into the ground. There was a small blast deflector on the muzzle. The weapon weighed 149kg and overall length was 2.87m with a 160cm-long barrel. Rate of fire was 10rds/min with a barrel life of 1,000 rounds. Effective range was 230m against moving targets and up to 500m for stationary targets to penetrate 160mm.

The *R-Werfer* was too heavy to manhandle on rough terrain. While it could be broken down into seven man-pack loads, it took too long to disassemble and reassemble. It is often said its advantage was that there was no back blast, but it created a large muzzle flash, smoke and dust cloud. The *R-Werfer* was used in Italy and on the Eastern Front. A few were found in Normandy accompanying units transferred from Italy. Most found by US troops were out of ammunition.

It is often thought that the ammunition for the *R-Werfer* and the *Panzerschreck* was interchangeable, and virtually every photo showing US troops posing with *R-Werfers* shows them with *Panzerschreck* rockets. In fact, the *Panzerschreck*'s RPzBGr 4322 was electrically initiated and

One of the few photos of the *R-Werfer* with its proper RPzBGr 4312 rocket, which had a tailboom approximately 75mm shorter than the *Panzerschreck*'s rocket. The double handgrips to the left of the breech block were used for traversing and elevating. There were no mechanical means for this. Simple iron sights were used rather than an optical sight. (Tom Laemlein/Armor Plate Press)

had a 650mm tailboom, while the RPzgr 4312 was initiated by a firing pin and percussion cap, and had a 490mm tailboom. The shaped-charge warheads and fusing were the same, however, and the reason 8.8cm calibre was selected for the *Panzerschreck* was because of the *R-Werfer*'s existing calibre. If the *R-Werfer* had not existed, the *Panzerschreck* might have been designed in a smaller calibre. The *R-Werfer* offered longer range than the *Panzerschreck*, but the *Panzerschreck* was much lighter, and faster and cheaper to produce.

## The M1 bazooka

The successful demonstration of the two models of the Pzf 30 at Kummersdorf in March 1943, described above, was followed by a demonstration of the American 2.36in M1 anti-tank rocket launcher, the 'bazooka'. These had been captured in Tunisia in November 1942 and were cruder than later bazooka models. Others were captured in Russia prior to this; 3,000 bazookas had been provided to the Soviets, and it was these that were first seen by the Germans. The Germans were impressed with the new weapon and it was decided to develop a counterpart. Development would be rushed, however, and many flaws emerged. It was more important to get an adequate anti-tank weapon into the hands of the troops rather than a fully perfected weapon.

The German counterpart of the bazooka would be larger in calibre by one-third than the American weapon, more robustly constructed, and used a more effective electrical firing system. In spite of its larger calibre and proportionally heavier shaped charge, it attained the same penetration but not quite the range of its American counterpart. The *Panzerschreck*'s effective range was 150–200m and could reach to 400m, but with little accuracy.

For years there has been confusion over the designation of the *Panzerschreck*. It is frequently called the 'RPzB 43', which is described as the first model without a blast shield. The next model was supposedly the RPzB 54, basically the 'RPzB 43' with a shield and minor improvements. The RPzB 54/1, with a much-shortened barrel, was stated to be a 'third' model.

In fact, the 'RPzB 43' and the RPzB 54 were the same weapon. It appears that 'RPzB 43' was a briefly used designation found in only one German manual. This was obtained by Allied intelligence and reported as the official designation in the US War Department's November 1944 *Intelligence Bulletin*. The shield was added later – in February 1944, well after the RPzB 54 designation was adopted – and the Western Allies made the assumption that with a shield it was a new model. In reality the weapon had been designated the RPzB 54 since September 1943 and the addition of the shield had no bearing on an assumed designation change. There was no such weapon as the 'RPzB 43' even though it is addressed in most books on German weapons. The US Army's March 1945 *Handbook on German Armed Forces* (TM-E 30-451) lists it as the Raketenpanzerbüchse 54.

In March 1943 the American 2.36in M1 anti-tank rocket launcher or 'bazooka' was demonstrated along with the two Pzf 30 models at Kummersdorf. This led to the development of the *Panzerschreck*. Here, the M6 rocket is painted yellow; from 1943 they were painted olive drab. (US Army)

## *Panzerschreck* and bazooka comparison

| Model | Calibre | Weight | Length | Range | Rate of fire |
|---|---|---|---|---|---|
| RPzB 54 | 8.8cm | 10.9kg* | 1,651mm | 200yd | 4–5rds/min |
| RPzB 54/1 | 8.8cm | 9.4kg | 1,350mm | 200yd | 4–5rds/min |
| M1A1** | 2.36in (60mm) | 13lb 3oz (5.9kg) | 54½in (1,386mm) | 250yd | 4–5rds/min |
| M9A1 | 2.36in (60mm) | 15lb 14oz (8.1kg) | 61in (1,550mm) | 300yd | 10rds/min |

*9.4kg without shield.

**The M1 and M9 bazookas had almost identical characteristics to the M1A1 and M9A1 respectively. The M9/M9A1 could be broken down into two sections for travel, each 31½in (800mm) long.

# THE *PANZERSCHRECK* DESCRIBED

## The projectile

The 8.8cm RPzBGr rocket was basically similar to the US 2.36in bazooka rocket. Most components were made of stampings. The 3.29kg rocket was 650mm long. The extended nipple-shaped nose cap had a point-detonating fuse. To provide the necessary stand-off, the nose cap was almost as long as the lower body, containing the shaped-charge liner (shaped like a bottle's shoulders and neck) and 0.66kg of *Pentol*. At the base of the warhead (*Geschoßkopf*) was the short adapter tube onto which the tailboom containing the rocket motor was fitted. Inside the adapter tube was a kleine Zündladung 34 as used in the *Panzerfaust*.

The 40mm-diameter tailboom combustion chamber (*Brennkammer*) contained six propellant sticks (*Treibladung*) in a bundle with a seventh in the centre. The sticks were 193mm long and 11mm in diameter with a

US soldiers examine RPzBGr 4322 rockets for the *Panzerschreck*. They could not be fired in the *R-Werfer*. While similar to the *R-Werfer*'s RPzBGr 4312 rocket, the latter had a percussion firing system (rather than electrical), a shorter tailboom, and different tailfin assembly. These soldiers are probably unable to decide what the *Panzerschreck* rocket's electrical firing wire is for. (Tom Laemlein/Armor Plate Press)

31

5.6mm central hole. A black-powder igniter pellet was at both ends of the central stick, through which a flash powder celluloid igniter tube ran. In the tail end was the rocket venturi (*Düse*), in which a Bakelite, cone-shaped electric rocket motor igniter (*Raketenmotoranzünder*) was glued. When this ignited, a flash of fire travelled up the igniter tube to ignite the pellet. The propellant sticks burned from front to rear to build up pressure better.

The tailfin assembly (*Leitwerk*) consisted of six vanes with a drum stabilizer. Two white insulated electrical wires emerged from the igniter with one soldered inside the fin drum as a ground. The other longer wire was attached to a single-prong plug (*Stecker*) fitted in an unpainted wooden handle (*Holzgriff*) with one concave curved edge. This was taped across the end of the fin assembly to protect the coiled electrical wires. The tape was used to bind the edge of the replacement glass pieces furnished in the rocket box for the shield's sighting window. The tape prevented the glass from cracking during firing. The plug was inserted in the launcher's contact box.

Upon detonation, the AZ5095/1 point-detonating fuse (*Aufschlagzünder*) fired a jet-like blast into the apex of the shaped-charge cone, which detonated the kleine Zündladung 34 embedded in the shaped charge's base. This was the major difference between the *Panzerfaust* and *Panzerschreck* shaped charges, the former with a base-detonating fuse and the latter with a point-detonating fuse. The point-detonating fuse was made safe by an arming pin (*Vorstecker*). This was actually an ill-suited fuse, being derived from the old rifle-grenade fuse with an arming pin added due to its sensitivity. The original fuse had been in production and was modified and available, even if not ideal.

There were three variants of the RPzBGr 4322 anti-tank rocket with seasonally adjusted propellant loads. The temperature ranges given below for the different rockets are 'standard', but they sometimes varied slightly owing to differences in propellant batches and were so marked on labels. The warmer the rocket propellant, the higher the firing pressure. Rockets unprotected from strong sunlight should not have been fired until they cooled down in the shade. Overheated rockets developed high ignition temperatures and the propellant could explode when ignited. Needless to say, this could be fatal to the crew as the maximum thrust was about 770kg with a pressure of 47.64MPa (6,910psi). Rockets exposed to extreme cold burned too slowly, leaving behind less completely consumed but still burning propellant particles. If possible, they were to be stored in warm bunkers or vehicles.

The first RPzBGr 4322 model was the Wintermunition 1943/44, designed for firing in a temperature range of -40 to +30°C. It was identified by 'Arkt' on the tailboom (short for *Arktisch* – 'arctic', also meaning winter). The Sommermunition 1944 was intended for -5 to +40–50°C (varied) and was not marked on the tailboom. The final rocket was the Wintermunition 1944/45, designed for a more realistic operating temperature range, -25 to +25°C. They were marked 'Arkt 44/45'. This model had a copper contact ring (*Kontaktring*) around the fin drum and a simplified contact plug. Troops used whatever rockets were available regardless of temperatures. Firing rockets in air temperatures outside of their specified range did not mean they were dangerous, but their performance would be affected, i.e., lower velocity and range, and degraded accuracy. A further improved, but never fielded, rocket was under development, the RPzBGr 4992, with the

# THE *PANZERSCHRECK* EXPOSED

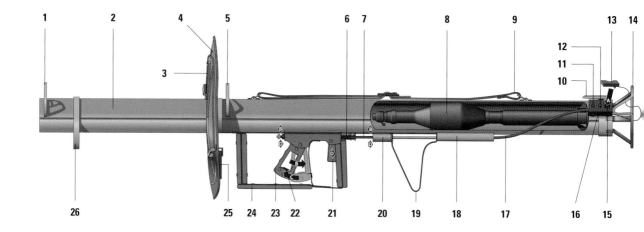

## 8.8cm RPzB 54 launcher (above) and 8.8cm RPzB 54/1 launcher (below)

1. Front sight (*Visiereinrichtung*)
2. Barrel (*Rohr*)
3. Sight port (*Glas*)
4. Shield (*Schutzschild*)
5. Rear sight (*Kimme*)
6. Spring
7. Punch rod (*Stoßstange*)
8. Rocket
9. Carrying sling (*Trageriemen*)
10. Latch (*Speere*)

11. Backstop bolt
12. Contact bolt
13. Missile connection plug
14. Breech guard (*Schutzkranz*)
15. Connector socket
16. Connector box (*Steckerkasten*)
17. Firing-wire tube (*Elektrische Abfeuereinrichtung*)
18. Shoulder rest (*Auflage*)
19. Shoulder support (*Stütze*)

20. Punch generator (*Stoßgenerator*)
21. Trigger (*Abzug*)
22. Safety release (*Sicherung*)
23. Cocking handle (*Spanngriff*)
24. Hand guard (*Handhabe*)
25. Replacement-window piece (*Ersatzglas*) bracket (*Behälter*)
26. Muzzle guard (*Schutzbügel*)

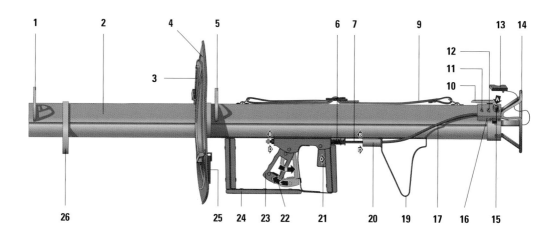

## 8.8cm RPzBGr 4322 rocket

1. Striker
2. Point-detonating fuse
3. Detonator
4. *Pentol* high-explosive filler
5. Booster charge (kleine Zündladung 34)
6. Igniter
7. Spacer
8. Propellant sticks
9. Trap ring
10. Electric primer fuse
11. Electric primer nozzle
12. Electric igniter wire
13. Tailfin assembly
14. Wing plates
15. Propellant tube
16. Primer
17. Shaped-charge cavity and liner
18. Nose cap
19. Arming pin

## Firing sequence

A. Rocket connection plugged into socket
B. Cocking handle squeezed, cocking punch rod, but held by notch, blocking trigger.
C. Cocking handle released, rod cocked, ready to fire.
D. Trigger squeezed, spring-loaded punch rod hits punch generator, inducing current that ignites rocket.

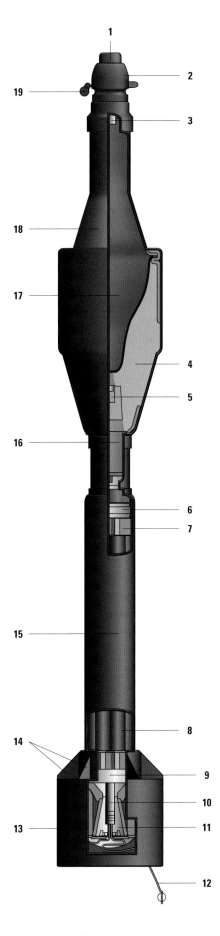

simpler and more reliable electrical contact system as used on the Wintermunition 1944/45.

There were two training rounds, the RPzBGr 4320Bl (*Blind-* or *Übungsgranate* – 'training projectile'), a target-practice rocket with an inert warhead and a live motor, and the RPzBGr 4329Ex (*Exerziergranate* – 'exercise projectile'), an exercise round with an inert warhead and motor for loading practice. The rocket warheads were painted Field Grey No. 3, a dark green, the tailboom phosphate green (*phosphatiert*) but usually field grey, and the drum fin assembly could be black or field grey. The model number was in black on the warhead's side and 'Arkt' in white on the tailboom of winter-loaded rockets.

## The launcher

The influence of the US bazooka can be seen in the more robust *Panzerschreck*. It consisted of a heavy steel 9.1cm-calibre barrel (*Rohr*) with three longitudinal pressed ridges running the bore's length to provide the 8.8cm calibre. The ridges, each approximately 1mm deep and 15mm wide, made it easier to manufacture, negating precise tolerances for the bore's full-length circumference; they reduced bore wear and friction, accommodated propellant fouling buildup and prevented small dents in the tube from blocking the bore. Being straight, the ridges did not impart a spin or otherwise stabilize the rocket. Barrel life was approximately 1,000 rounds.

On the left side of the muzzle was the front sight (*Visiereinrichtung* or *Korn*). Behind this, on the barrel's bottom side, was the muzzle guard (*Schutzbügel*), a bracket to help prevent dirt, mud and snow from entering when resting the weapon on a trench parapet. The detachable protective shield (*Schutzschild*) – if present – was fitted on the left side immediately forward of the rear sight (*Kimme*). The shield was secured to the left side of the barrel with a metal constriction band and latch. There was a small blast-proof glass window (termed *Glas*, but actually made of mica) for sighting. Near the bottom was a bracket (*Behälter*) for a replacement window piece (*Ersatzglas*). Three small brackets on the shield's front were for attaching camouflage.

The handle (*Handhabe*) was a strap metal handguard with wood grips that mounted and protected the firing mechanism, comprised of the cocking handle (*Spanngriff*), safety release (*Sicherung*) and trigger (*Abzug*). To the rear of this was the metal shoulder support (*Stütze*), a curved metal strap, and the shoulder rest (*Auflage*), a metal cover also protecting the electrical firing wires (*Elektrische Abfeuereinrichtung*), housed in a contoured steel tube. The punch generator (*Stoßgenerator*) was housed in a steel cup forward of the shoulder support. The generator looked like a C cell battery. This was connected to the two firing wires.

The firing mechanism was a spring-loaded, 274mm-long horizontal punch rod (*Stoßstange*) set in the upper portion of the handle. Its securing nut was spot-welded in place, signifying that it did not have to be adjusted or the punch generator replaced. The firing wires ran to the connector box (*Steckerkasten*) at the 10 o'clock position (when viewed from the breech looking forward) on the breech. The rocket's electrical firing wires were plugged into this. At the 12 o'clock position over the breech was the latch

(*Speere*) that held the loaded rocket in position. Around the breech was a heavy-gauge wire protective guard (*Schutzkranz*) that helped keep out dirt and mud and guided the rocket when being loaded. An adjustable web carrying sling (*Trageriemen*) was fixed to the top of the barrel.

## PANZERSCHRECK VARIANTS

### The RPzB 54

This first *Panzerschreck* model, the RPzB 54, began to be fielded in October 1943 after production began in September. The first weapons were rushed to the Eastern Front where the Soviets had launched a major offensive in August and were battering their way west in spite of Hitler's *Haltebefehl* ('stand fast order'). The weapon was fielded with flaws and it was not long before recommendations for improvements arrived from the field.

The most significant problem was the incomplete burning of the rocket propellant in the barrel. The rocket continued to burn for up to 2m *after* leaving the muzzle, especially in cold temperatures. This caused burning propellant particles to be blown back at the firer, causing serious face and hand burns. This was not an occasional occurrence, but assured. For protection, firers were to wear a steel helmet, M30 or M38 gasmask with the snout filter removed, and gloves. Even a hood of some sort was recommended to protect the ears and sides of the head – field caps had folded side curtains that could be pulled down for head protection. (This same problem existed with the American bazooka, but to a much lesser extent. They provided a facemask with the bazooka and recommended helmet and gloves.)

Units sometimes fabricated simple rectangular or circular shields. Plans were issued for a locally fabricated 37cm×40cm shield. All shields were required to be detachable. A factory-made 36cm×47cm protective shield (*Schutzschild*) was issued in February 1944 to retrofit on fielded *Panzerschrecke* and added to new-production weapons. There were two variants, but these were only minor manufacturers' differences. It held a small window for sighting, but it restricted observation and made target acquisition

Northern France, 31 July 1944: British soldiers look over a *Panzerschreck*. Here, the shield is positioned too far forward. It should be just forward of the rear sight, which the leftmost soldier is touching. Unpainted rocket ammunition boxes marked 'R.Mun. 4322' in black can be seen on the ground to the left. (© IWM B 8311)

difficult. The shield possessed a gap on the right side of the barrel's cut-out, making the firer's right hand vulnerable. He still had to wear a glove. An add-on hand-protection plate (*Handschutz*) was retrofitted to some shields.

The troops found the RpzB 54 awkward to handle, especially in the close confines of field fortifications. It was easy for dirt, mud and snow to enter the muzzle. In an effort to reduce this, a bracket-like muzzle guard (*Schutzbügel*) was fitted under

Aiming a *Panzerschreck*. This view provides details of the blast shield, including the three camouflage attachment brackets. The muzzle protector is also shown. The barrel's longitudinal corrugations can also be seen. While the weapon appears new, it may have been freshly repainted as the web sling shows a high degree of wear. The slings were rather flimsy. (Tom Laemlein/Armor Plate Press)

the muzzle in February 1944 and on all new-production weapons. A problem was discovered with the mounting brackets attaching the breech's circular protective guard (*Schutzkranz*). The rocket's warhead possessed a 'step' in the body's design that caught on the breech's rim, causing it to hang up for a potentially fatal moment. Metal strips were riveted or welded on the inside of the brackets or a weld-bead added to the end of each bracket at the breech rim to eliminate the hang-up. The front and rear sights were initially too fragile and replaced by more robust designs; these new sights were adjustable for windage and for summer- and winter-loaded rockets. The sights were improved in early and mid-1944 with the two subsequent versions possessing improved adjustments for zeroing and temperature-range accommodation. A simplified safety release was introduced in late 1944. From January/February 1944, new-production *Panzerschrecke* included these modifications and many in the field were altered through a series of directives, including issue modification kits. These fully modified *Panzerschrecke* were produced until August 1944.

## The RPzB 54/1

The RPzB 54/1 was developed in late 1944. It was not manufactured, but depot-converted from existing stocks of the RPzB 54. The most noticeable modification was the barrel being shortened (*verkürtze*) by 340mm. The long, ungainly barrel of the original *Panzerschreck* was necessary to reduce the burning propellant blowback hazard, which burned for about 3.5m to include inside the barrel, but did little to increase range. The addition of the shield negated the need for a long barrel. The section of barrel to be removed was taken from the breech end, rather than the muzzle as would be assumed. The *Heerestechnisches Verordnungsblatt* ('Army Technical Gazette') of 15 January 1945 directed that units would begin receiving the shortened RPzB 54/1 to replace the longer weapons, which were to be turned into depots, refitted and reissued. Weight was reduced by 1.5kg. With the weight of the loaded rocket directly over the firer's shoulder, and the bulk of the barrel, firing mechanism and shield forward, it was fairly well balanced. Once fired, however, it was front heavy.

The modification steps included: sling removed; paint stripped; shoulder rest removed; electrical firing wire tube removed; 34cm cut off of breech end; front and rear sights replaced; new zeroing marks added; new rear sling swivel welded on; new contact holes drilled in the top of the barrel near the breech end; improved contact box for old and new type rockets refitted to the 12 o'clock position (from 10 o'clock); improved easier loading rocket latch refitted to 2 o'clock position (from 12 o'clock); new reinforced protective breech guard welded on with seven or ten brackets (manufacturers' differences), designed to eliminate the step that rockets caught on, replacing the original six; new shortened electrical firing wire tube fitted, to the right rather than the left side; hand guard added to the shield; weapon repainted dark yellow; sling attached; and the sights zeroed to the bore. Not all earlier modifications were applied to all reworked *Panzerschrecke*. For example, refitted RPzB 54/1s were not always fitted with the improved safety release or new sights.

A total of 107,450 RPzB 54s were turned in from January 1945, but only 25,744 rebuilt RPzB 54/1s were delivered by March. RPzB 54s remained in wide use to the war's end.

## *PANZERSCHRECK* PRODUCTION

Although the weapon was developed by HASAG Meuselwitz, *Panzerschreck* production was undertaken by other firms: Enzinger-Union-Werke AG, Mannheim (clu); Schricker & Company, Fürth-Vach, Bahnhof, Bayern (kxs); and HASAG Eisen- und Metallwerke GmbH, Werk Tschenstochau in Poland (nbe). Shields were made by Enzinger-Union-Werke – also producing *Panzerschrecke* – and H. W. Schmidt, Metallwaren Döbeln (brg44). In 1943, 50,835 *Panzerschrecke* were produced, followed by 238,316 in 1944 and 25,744 in 1945, making a total of 314,895. For comparison, the United States produced almost 395,000 bazookas of all models.

Three firms loaded and assembled *Panzerschreck* rockets while more than a dozen others made components. Total rocket production was 2,218,400. For comparison, the United States produced 15,603,000 bazooka rockets.

# USE
## Hunting tanks

### PRECURSORS IN GERMAN SERVICE

To get a sense of the revolutionary impact the advent of the *Panzerfaust* and *Panzerschreck* had on German anti-tank doctrine after 1942, it is necessary to assess the existing types of anti-armour weaponry fielded by Germany's infantry during World War II.

### Towed anti-tank weapons

In 1939–42, the Wehrmacht relied on several conventional light anti-tank weapons. Twelve guns were allotted to the *Infanterie-Regiment*'s three-platoon anti-armour company and 36 to the divisional anti-armour battalion. These large, heavy weapons were difficult to conceal, required much work to dig in, and were slow to relocate to new positions, essential if they were to survive. They were also expensive and time-consuming to build,

The principal anti-tank gun in the first three years of the conflict was the Rheinmetall-Borsig 3.7cm PaK 35/36. Considered one of the world's best anti-tank weapons in the mid-1930s and copied by many countries, by 1940 it was obsolescent. Derisively called the *Türklopfer* ('doorknocker') or *Panzeranklopfgerät* ('armour-knocking equipment'), it was operated by a six-man crew and towed by a light field truck. The PaK 35/36's original PaK Pzgr round could penetrate 40mm at 400m. In 1940 the 3.7cm PaK Pzgr 40 round was introduced, penetrating 50mm at 400m. In 1941 the Stielgranate 41 – a massive muzzle-loaded shaped-charge stick grenade, essentially a very large 'rifle grenade' – was developed in order to extend the gun's life. It had a 159mm warhead capable of penetrating 150mm with an effective range of 185m, though longer ranges could be achieved. (Cody Images)

requiring sophisticated manufacturing facilities and materials essential for tanks and artillery.

The 5cm PaK 38 was first fielded in late 1940 to replace the inadequate PaK 35/36. The PaK 38 mainly equipped regimental anti-tank companies, but often there was a mix of 3.7cm and 5cm guns. With a good shot with the PaK Pzgr 40 it could knock out the feared Soviet T-34 tank. This round penetrated 85mm at 500m while the standard PaK Pzgr round penetrated 60mm. Production continued until mid-1944. The PaK 38 was succeeded by the 7.5cm PaK 40, first fielded in late 1941 but not seeing widespread use until 1942. This became the main divisional anti-armour gun, but some were assigned to regimental anti-armour companies. Heavy to manhandle, it nevertheless proved to be an effective weapon. It could knock out most tanks, penetrating 105mm at 500m with the PaK Pzgr round and 115mm with the PaK Pzgr 40 round. The Germans were so desperately in need of anti-tank guns they employed just about all captured weapons, but numbers were still insufficient. After the Axis invasion of the Soviet Union in June 1941, many captured Soviet 76.2mm FS-22 guns were re-chambered for the longer German 7.5cm round and further modified for anti-tank use as the 7.62cm PaK 36(r) – keeping the original 7.62cm designation. It was common for 5cm, 7.5cm and 7.62cm guns to be mixed in units.

These towed anti-tank guns were heavy and difficult to relocate to a new firing position, a practice essential for survival. Even the 3.7cm weighed 432kg. The 5cm weighed twice as much and the 7.5cm weighed almost four times as much. The popular converted Russian 7.62cm was even heavier. Manhandling such heavy weapons to new positions became problematic and virtually impossible under fire without a prime-mover.

## Man-portable weapons

At platoon level, rifle-grenade launchers were allocated one per infantry section. Regardless of the increasingly larger calibre of their shaped-charge warheads, they were only marginally effective against light armour, and lacked accuracy. First issued in 1940, the GG/P 40 used a spigot-type launcher. The grenade was ineffective even though the Germans used a base-detonating fuse; it lacked the necessary stand-off in the form of a nosecone to improve the effectiveness of the shaped charge, and was withdrawn in 1942.

Introduced in early 1942, the first *Gewehr Panzergranate* ('rifle [anti-] armour grenade') was a 30mm shaped charge offering 20–30mm penetration and with an effective range of 50–100m. By the end of 1942, the 40mm *große Gewehrpanzergranate*, an over-calibre

The 7.9mm Kar 98k carbine, the standard infantryman's weapon, fitted with the cup-type discharger (*Schießbecher*) and the clip-on auxiliary rear sight (*Hilfsvisier*). Before it to the left lies the yellow-bodied 30mm *Gewehr Sprenggranate* ('rifle high-explosive grenade') that could be used as a hand grenade with a pull friction igniter in the base, along with a disassembled example. In the centre is a *Gewehr Sprenggranate, Weitschuss* ('rifle high explosive grenade, long-range') with a black body. To the right is a *Gewehr Panzergranate* ('rifle anti-armour grenade') with a black body. Its effective range was 50m with a 50mm penetration under ideal conditions and angle of impact. (Tom Laemlein/Armor Plate Press)

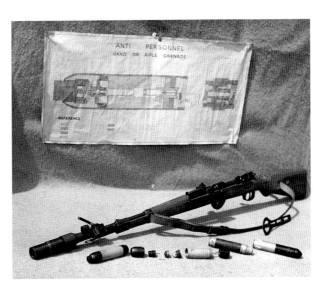

El Agheila, Libya, April 1941: this German soldier mans a PzB 39. Capable of penetrating 30mm at 100m, the 7.9mm ammunition used in the PzB 39 and its precursor, the PzB 38, was loaded in a 94mm-long, high-capacity case. Only 1,600 of the complex and expensive semi-automatic PzB 38 were produced, while 39,232 of the less costly, single-shot PzB 39 were built. The bullet was too small to do much damage, ricocheting around the inside of a tank if it penetrated. The PzB 38 weighed 15.99kg and the PzB 39 was 12.43kg. (Cody Images)

grenade capable of penetrating 50mm at ranges of up to 150m, was introduced. The 46mm and 61mm versions were introduced in late 1942 and late 1943 respectively, with an effective range of 80–100m. The 46mm penetrated 70–90mm and the 61mm pierced 100–120mm.

In the early part of World War II Germany's infantry was also armed with the bipod-mounted PzB 38 and PzB 39 anti-tank rifles. Each rifle company had a seven-man section with three such rifles. One could be attached to each platoon, but it was preferred to keep them grouped for concentrated fire. These anti-tank rifles were obsolete by the end of the French campaign, although some remained in use into 1944 in secondary roles. Their inadequacy was recognized early and in 1939/40 Waffenfabrik Wilhelm Gustloff Werke in Weimar successfully converted the PzB 39 to fire anti-tank rifle grenades, resulting in the GrB 39. Between March 1940 and November 1941 (most sources incorrectly say 1942), most were converted, and the GrB 39 would remain in use to the war's end. The barrel was shortened to 590mm, the bipod was extended 53mm to allow increased elevation in order to achieve the necessary grenade range, the shoulder stock was reinforced and was no longer foldable, the forearm removed, a cup-type grenade discharger fixed, and special sights fitted. The rear sight provided lead marks for tracking a moving tank. Different rear-sight inserts were provided for each model of grenade.

The 10.5kg, 1,224mm-long GrB 39 projected standard anti-armour rifle grenades to a longer range, 150m. However, it was only accurate against moving targets up to 75m. It fired the larger 40mm, 46mm and 61mm *Gewehr Panzergranaten*. It used the massive 7.9×94mm Treibpatrone 318 ('318 propelling cartridge') with a round-nose wooden bullet. The GrB 39 replaced the obsolete 7.9mm anti-armour rifles, with three notionally issued per rifle company, although many units did not receive them. The three rifles were consolidated into a *Granatbüchse-Trupp* ('grenade rifle troop'), either to be employed as a single element for concentrated fires against tanks or with one to be attached to each rifle platoon. Obviously the GrB 39 was inadequate, offering limited range and penetration for a weapon of its weight – less than 1.5kg lighter than the MG 34, the standard-issue section light machine gun.

## Anti-armour grenades

The Germans did not adopt anti-armour hand grenades until late 1942. Such grenades were desperate measures and not widely used. The principal German hand-delivered anti-tank weapon was the 3kg Haft-Hl3 (Haft-Hohlladung 3kg – *Haft* means to cling – or 'magnetic hollow charge 3kg'). Known as the *Panzerknacker* ('armour-cracker'), it was adopted in November 1942. It was a truncated cone-shaped device with a handle holding the fuse with three pairs of magnets allowing it to be attached to a tank turret or hull, gun cupola, pillbox doors or embrasure shutters. Early models had a 4.5-second delay friction igniter, which sometimes did not allow time for the attacker to seek cover. A 7.5-second delay fuse was introduced in May 1943. The Haft-Hl3 could penetrate up to 140mm of armour and 500mm of concrete.

The later Haft-Hl3,5 (Haft-Hohlladung 3, 5kg) was essentially the same as the Haft-Hl3, but the truncated cone-shaped body was replaced by a Pzf 60 warhead with the nose cap removed, giving it a 180mm penetration. It used the same plywood base, three pairs of magnets, and

Normandy, 26 June 1944: a British sapper displays a Haft-Hl3. Adopted in November 1942, the *Panzerknacker* was officially replaced by the *Panzerfaust* in May 1944. (© IWM B 6015)

7.5-second delay fuse as the Haft-Hl3. The standard kleine Zündladung 34 ('small booster charge 1934') was retained. It saw very limited use before it and other versions of the *Haft-Hohlladungen* were declared obsolete on 15 May 1944 to be replaced by existing models of the *Panzerfaust*, although the on-hand charges remained in use. Captured 'armour-crackers' were widely used by the Red Army, which is why the Germans applied *Zimmerit* anti-magnetic plaster to their tanks and assault guns.

## ISSUE AND DEPLOYMENT

The *Panzerfaust* was issued as a round of ammunition in the same manner as the hand grenade. In combat, *Panzerfäuste* were issued to selected soldiers as needed. In the defence, one to three might be found in a two-man fighting position or machine-gun nest, depending on whether the terrain was deemed armour-proof (*Panzerschier*) or armour-feasible (*Panzermöglich*). It was common for a mix of models to be found in units. For example, a unit might receive both the Pzf 30 (klein) and the Pzf 30 (groß), along with the Pzf 60. They took whatever was available.

There was an official allocation of *Panzerfäuste* to units, but like anything else in the Wehrmacht, with its transport and distribution difficulties, these were only guidelines. Heer and Waffen-SS units followed the same issue guidelines. Each rifle and *Pionier* (combat engineer) company was to receive 36, while anti-tank companies and other divisional company-size units each received 18, and artillery batteries 12. These allocations were

December 1944: *Volksgrenadier* personnel train with the *Panzerschreck*. In the *Volksgrenadier-Divisionen*, raised from August 1944 onwards, the infantry *Panzerjäger* function was carried out by each *Volksgrenadier*-Regiment's 14. Panzer-Zerstörer-Kompanie ('tank-destroyer company'). These divisions fielded fewer personnel than their predecessors and were equipped for defensive warfare; their designation ('people's grenadier') was intended to boost morale. (Cody Images)

for *Infanterie-Divisionen, Volksgrenadier-Divisionen, Jäger-Divisionen* and *Gebirgs-Divisionen*, totalling about 2,000 per division.

Unlike the *Panzerfaust*, the *Panzerschreck* was issued to a dedicated two-man crew (*Schützen für Panzerbüchse*), comprising a gunner (*Richtschütze*) and a loader (*Ladeschütze*). Early on, some units issued two or three per rifle company, but these were ordered to be removed since *Panzerfäuste* were available. During World War II, each of the infantry division's infantry regiments (from 1942 redesignated *Grenadier-Regimenter*) fielded an integral 14. Panzerjäger-Kompanie ('tank-hunter company'), armed with 9–12 anti-tank guns, which was not assigned to one of the regiment's rifle battalions. (In German usage, company numbers ran consecutively through the regiment, meaning I. Bataillon fielded 1.–4. Kompanien, II. Bataillon included 5.–8. Kompanien, and so on. From late 1944 most *Grenadier-Regimenter* possessed only two battalions; even so, the anti-tank company retained its traditional numbering. In December 1944 the *Infanterie-Division 45* organization, intended to supplant all existing tables of organization, was established and – at least in theory – the *Panzerjäger-Kompanien* were converted to *Panzer-Zerstörer-Kompanien*.)

This company was armed primarily with 54 *Panzerschrecke* (plus a further 18 in reserve; no doubt some units parcelled out the reserve *Panzerschrecke* to other units) but also possessing 90 *Panzerfäuste*. It had a small headquarters; a supply train (*Troß*), including baggage and ammunition transport, a field kitchen, and 18 spare *Panzerschrecke*; and three *Panzer-Zerstörer-Züge* ('tank-destroyer platoons'). This is assuming the company possessed a full complement of *Panzerschrecke*; in many cases they had far less. It was not uncommon for such companies to field only two platoons. Some companies possessed two *Panzerschreck* platoons and a third platoon retaining three 7.5cm towed anti-tank guns to provide long-range fires. Just prior to this some units received 48 *Panzerschrecke* while retaining the *Panzerjäger-Kompanie* designation.

A *Panzer-Zerstörer-Zug* consisted of a platoon troop (*Zugtrupp*), including the platoon commander, troop leader (platoon sergeant),

messenger, two-man machine-gun crew, and a horse-handler with a pair of horse-drawn infantry carts. There were three 14-man *Panzer-Zerstörer-Gruppen* ('tank-destroyer squads'), each including a squad leader, two troop leaders (doubling as gunners), four gunners, six loaders, and one horse-handler with a horse and two If 8 infantry carts (see page 52). The group was in turn organized into two six-man *Panzer-Zerstörer-Truppen* ('tank-destroyer troops'), each manning three *Panzerschrecke*.

A troop's three crews normally operated in unison, covering the same area or avenue of approach. The gunners were armed with pistols, the loaders and horse-handler with carbines, and the squad leader with a submachine gun. Besides operating three *Panzerschrecke*, they functioned as tank-hunters (*Panzerjagdtruppe*) to 'blind, halt, and destroy' enemy armour. They were additionally prescribed five *Panzerfäuste* and/or magnetic hand-charges, 20 smoke pots, a rifle-grenade launcher with anti-tank and anti-personnel grenades, and several smoke hand grenades.

Beyond the Heer's infantry regiments several types of specialist units were armed with *Panzerschrecke*. Twelve *Panzer-Zerstörer-Bataillone (teilmotorisiert)* ('tank-destroyer battalions (partly motorized)') – 470–479, 485 and 486 – were raised as army- and army-group-level troops in the autumn of 1943 on the Eastern Front. Manned by infantrymen, each battalion contained a battalion staff and three *Panzer-Zerstörer-Kompanien* (tank-destroyer companies) organized as below. The battalions were employed to block enemy breakthroughs, or parcelled out as individual companies to divisions – or regiments within a division – in the defence. They were used to increase the depth of the defence by digging in multiple positions, covering roads and other avenues of approach. There were also some *selbständige Panzer-Zerstörer-Kompanien (bespannt)* ('separate tank destroyer companies (cart transport)'), raised in early 1944.

In contrast to the various types of foot-mobile division fielded by the Heer, *Panzer-Divisionen* and *Panzergrenadier-Divisionen* fielded fewer infantry and so were issued 1,000 and 1,500 *Panzerfäuste*, respectively. Officially, *Panzer-* and *Panzergrenadier-Divisionen* were not issued

## Colours and markings

Throughout the Wehrmacht, dark yellow (*dunkelgelb*, called 'ordnance yellow' or 'Panzer yellow' by collectors) – a dark tan with variations in shade – had been adopted in February 1943 to paint munitions, field equipment and vehicles with a light base colour for over-painting camouflage and to conserve green pigment. It replaced the former field grey (*feldgrau*), a dark green that varied greatly in shade.

### Panzerfäuste

Since they were single-use weapons, *Panzerfäuste* were not painted in camouflaging colours by the units employing them. *Panzerfäuste* did not appear weathered, scratched, scraped or worn from use. They were typically uncrated factory-fresh and used within a short time. The actual colours of *Panzerfäuste* varied and have long been a subject of debate. There was no one standard paint colour or set of markings. Most were dark yellow, but *Panzerfäuste* were also painted with a brighter yellow-brown (*gelbbraun*), sand grey (*sandgrau*), and occasionally dark green (*dunkelgrun*). There are photographic examples with the lower portion of the warhead a dark colour (probably green) and the nose cap and tube dark yellow. The spring steel collar securing the tailboom to the warhead was usually black, but sometimes the same colour as the tube. The folding fins were painted black or left unpainted. The waterproof paper cap on the breech was black or dark brown. The Finns over-painted most of their *Panzerfäuste* dark green.

Cautionary warning markings were usually decals (transfers), with dull-red lettering on a dark-yellow background, even if the tube was painted green or another colour. Markings were also stencilled. There were many variations in markings. The same applied to paper instruction labels on the warhead, with illustrations and printed word styles varying. The red warnings on the right side of the tube appeared 'upside-down' when viewed from the side, but were readable to the gunner as he looked down at it while holding it to his right side. Not all of the following decals/stencilling were necessarily applied to all *Panzerfäuste*. From front to rear, they read: 'Starker Feuerstrahl!' ('Strong jet of fire!'), with a forwards-pointing arrowhead; 'Vorsicht!' ('Caution!'), on the middle portion of the tube; 'Starker Feuerstrahl!' ('Strong jet of fire!'), with a rearwards-pointing arrowhead.

On the other side of the tube was the warning: 'Vorsicht! Rohr ist immer mit Pulver geladen auch wenn Geschoß – kopf abgenommen und Flügelhalter herausgezogen!' ('Caution! Tube is always loaded with powder even if projectile head and fin holder are removed!'). After 'Vorsicht!', the rest of the text was displayed in two lines. Small decals *may* have been applied to the trigger lever – 'Feuer' ('Fire'), and on the right side of the tube beside the safety slide – 'Entsichert' ('Unlocked'). The sight's apertures usually had the range stamped beside them and stencilled in red, black or green.

A black-on-white printed label was glued to the lower side of the warhead. Labels were often varnished, giving them a tan tint. They depicted an illustration of a soldier holding a *Panzerfaust* in an underarm firing position with a warning about the back blast (*Vorsicht*) along with its designation, for example, 'Panzerfaust 60m'. Below this were listed step-by-step instructions for preparing the warhead for firing:

1. Kopf abnehmen. ('Remove the [war]head.')
2. Kopf senkrecht halten u. Zündlung 34 so einsetzen, daß das Papier-Abdeckblatt sichtbar ist. ('Hold head upright and insert booster charge 34 so that the paper cover is visible.')
3. Zünder einsetzen mit dem Zündhütchen gegen das Papier-Abdeckblatt. ('Insert fuse with the primer against the paper cover.')
4. Kopf wieder aufstecken. ('Attach the head again.')
5. Die Pappkappe am Rohrende bleibt beim Abschuß aufgesetzt. ('The cardboard cap on tube end stays put during firing.')

**ABOVE** Finnish soldiers prepare to fire the Pzf 30 (groß). The Finns usually over-painted their *Panzerfäuste* dark green, but these are the original German dark yellow. The far man is cocking the firing mechanism. On the near *Panzerfaust* the red-painted trigger button is on the forward end of the firing mechanism and aft of the raised sight. (Tom Laemlein/Armor Plate Press)

and three-colour patterns using the dark-yellow base colour and adding varied shades of green and brown, either brushed or spray-painted. This is called 'Normandy camouflage' by collectors, but was not restricted to that region. They were sometimes whitewashed in winter, and quickly showed worn spots from handling. Whitewash could be scrubbed off in the spring – with traces remaining – and/or over-painted with a new solid or camouflage pattern.

The inside of the tube was unpainted, requiring it to be lightly oiled, but it was common for some of the spray paint to have coated the inside of the muzzle and breech. The connector box at the breech end could be primer red, black, or painted over with dark yellow or one of the camouflaging colours. The cocking lever and trigger were usually dark yellow, olive green (*olivgrün*), or bare metal, with the assumption it would be worn off anyway. The web sling was tan or light brown.

Manufacturer's codes were usually stamped on the bottom of the trigger guard (clu, kxs, nbe) as well as somewhere on the shield (brg44, clu) along with a *Waffenamt Abnahmestempel* (WaA, or 'Weapon Office Acceptance Mark'). The launchers' and shields' manufacturers were often different. Oddly, there were no serial numbers. Serial numbers were applied to *Panzerschrecke* used by the Finnish Army, a three- or four-digit number stamped near the manufacturer's mark.

### Panzerschrecke

Virtually all *Panzerschrecke* were factory-painted dark yellow over a coat of dark-red primer (*oxidrot*). Wooden handgrips were also painted. Any found in other colours were repainted by the unit. What appear to be solid dark green (*dunkelgrun*) and dark grey (*dunkelgrau*) *Panzerschrecke* are seen in black-and-white photos. Units frequently camouflage-painted *Panzerschrecke* in various two-

*Panzerschrecke*. Regardless, some *Panzergrenadier* units obtained a few. Battalions assigned as corps-level troops received 50 *Panzerfäuste* each and those operating under GHQ about 70.

The Luftwaffe issued *Panzerschrecke* to most units of its *Fallschirmjäger-Divisionen*, not just anti-tank units. Each of the parachute division's three parachute regiments received 54; the divisional headquarters was allocated six; the anti-tank battalion got 36, the artillery regiment and anti-aircraft battalion 12 each, the reconnaissance company four, and the mortar, pioneer and signal battalions each received six.

## OPERATING THE *PANZERFAUST*

The *Panzerfaust* was designed for simplicity of operation. Warhead preparation instructions were printed on a label on the warhead and cautionary warnings marked on the launcher tube (see page 46). The two Pzf 30 models operated the same, while the Pzf 60 and Pzf 100 operated in a different manner from the two Pzf 30 models.

### Selecting a firing position

The firer had to make certain he had a clear area to his rear, as the flash and blast could be fatal. There was a flash of flame to the rear at least 3m long, meaning that firing the *Panzerfaust* required an area 3m deep to be clear of personnel, equipment, flammable materials, and anything that could reflect the back blast. This included walls, board fences, rear parapets of trenches and foxholes, trees or any other obstruction. Reflected back blast would cause serious injuries to the firer and nearby personnel. Special attention had to be given when firing from the prone posture so

A rearguard position on a ridge side with a Pzf 30 (klein). Hacked-down weeds help camouflage the position. Note the lack of a parapet. Spoil was often carted away to make the position less conscious and provide a clear area to the rear for the *Panzerfaust*'s back blast. (Nik Cornish at www.stavka.org.uk)

that the firer's legs were well to the side, out of the back blast's path. If the launcher was angled too high when firing from the standing or kneeling position the blast could be reflected into the legs, along with gravel or other debris kicked up by the blast.

It is often said that *Panzerfäuste* could not be fired from within buildings. This was not true. If there was a clear area at least 3m deep to the rear and an open door or large window anywhere in the room – preferably near the back-blast path – it could be fired. The *Panzerfaust* warhead was armed upon firing, so could not be fired through undergrowth, tree limbs or windowpanes. The firer had to ensure the flight path was clear of obstructions. For longer-ranged shots it was recommended that the firer lean against a building corner, tree or any solid support for a steady aim.

## Preparing the warhead

The first step was to prepare the warhead for firing. The *Panzerfaust* was taken from the box. A carton contained four booster charges and primers, and one of each was removed. The spring steel clip on the lower portion of the warhead was unclipped from the retaining collar on the upper end of the tailboom and the warhead detached. Holding the warhead nose-down, the smaller booster charge was inserted into the tail tube so its paper cover was visible; it was followed by the larger primer. If the booster was inserted upside down the projectile would not detonate. Still holding the warhead nose-down, the soldier reinserted it into the launcher tube; the clip locked to the retaining collar. The paper cap on the breech was left in place.

## Firing postures

Soldiers were taught to fire the *Panzerfaust* from the right underarm or right shoulder, but there was no reason it could not be fired from the left shoulder/side. *Panzerfäuste* were most often photographed being fired from the underarm position, but it was common to fire them from atop the shoulder. It all depended on what was necessary to ensure a clear area behind the launcher for the back blast. Four example firing positions were shown in manuals applicable to all models. These were: within a fighting position (foxhole, trench), with the weapon atop the shoulder; kneeling position, with the weapon under the arm; kneeling or standing position in an unrestricted area, with the weapon atop the shoulder; and prone, with the weapon atop the shoulder.

A grenadier awaits action in a slit trench. Since the soil was piled behind the position, he would have to fire the Pzf 60 in an over-the-shoulder position rather than the customary underarm position to clear the rear parapet or more formally, the parados. To the side lie an MP 44 assault rifle and Gew 43 self-loading rifle. (Tom Laemlein/Armor Plate Press)

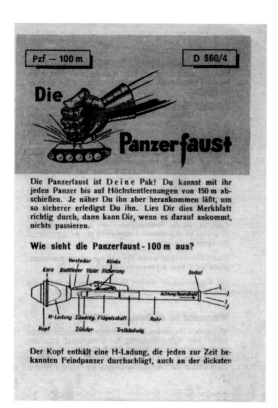

While not a prescribed firing position, contemporary film footage shows soldiers firing the *Panzerfaust* by holding it with two hands, with the tube on top of the forearm and held in the crook of the arm. If fired from under the arm or in the crook of the arm, the left hand gripped under the tube just behind the muzzle and the right hand gripped the tube at the trigger lever with the thumb atop the trigger. When the *Panzerfaust* was fired from the shoulder, the left hand gripped behind the muzzle and the right hand was atop the tube, with the fingers over the trigger and the thumb hooked below the tube.

## Firing the *Panzerfaust*

With the Pzf 60 and Pzf 100 the safety pin was pulled from the right side to release the sight, which was raised by hand. The locking rod inside the trigger lever was pushed forward towards the sight and locked. The selected range's aperture was aligned with the foresight bead on the top rim of the warhead and both were aligned on the target. To fire, the trigger lever was smoothly and firmly pressed and the weapon fired. It required little pressure.

Both models of the earlier Pzf 30 operated differently from later models, but the booster and primer were loaded in the same manner. The Pzf 30 firing mechanism consisted of a small tube about 180mm long welded to the top of the launcher tube. In the forward end was a thin square rod with the striker on the rear end. The forward end of the rod ran through a vertical red-painted trigger button protruding from the tube's top forward end. A spring was coiled around the square rod. When

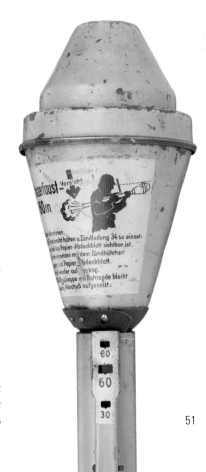

the sight was raised after pulling out the latch pin, the spring pushed the rod's forward end out of the tube's end and it was cocked. On the rear end was a protruding sleeve with a small red-painted stud. The sleeve prevented the striker from hitting the primer. The stud was rotated to the left and the spring-loaded sleeve cleared the primer, making it ready to fire. When the trigger button was pressed, the striker rod was released, the primer fired, and the propellant charge detonated.

Upon firing, regardless of the model, there was a sharp crack with considerable flash and a white smoke cloud to the rear as well as kicked-up dust. There was a smaller smoke cloud to the front and at night a significant muzzle flash was noticeable, but not so much in daylight. There was no recoil, but the immediate departure of the warhead caused the launcher to jerk slightly upwards.

If the *Panzerfaust* was not immediately fired, the primer and booster could be removed and returned to the box. The slide bar was uncocked, the sight lowered, and the safety pin reinserted, making the *Panzerfaust* safe to transport. If it misfired, the warhead was to be removed and the weapon turned in. In the reality of combat, they were most often simply discarded in a still armed state.

## Hitting the target

When fired the *Panzerfaust*'s projectile's flight could easily be seen, as it appeared like an American football, which had a typical velocity of just slightly less than a Pzf 30 projectile. The *Panzerfaust* penetrated up to

## *Panzerfaust* and *Panzerschreck* carriage

*Panzerfäuste* were shipped four to a wooden box, which was usually painted some shade of green or left unpainted. The top-opening boxes used for most models measured 1,092×457×178mm with 'Panzerfaust' stencilled on the lip and usually the front side, in very small to very large black lettering. There were rope carrying handles on the ends, two hinges and two latches on the lid. Inside were two wooden spacers with notches for four weapons laid in the box with the warhead ends alternating. The Pzf 30 (klein) box measured 1,041×305×15mm and was marked 'Panzerfaust (klein)'. The boxes contained four each of the kleine Zündladung 34 and *Faustpatronezünder* ('first cartridge primer', with three variants – FPZ 8001, FPZ 8002 and FPZ 8003 – being available) in a cardboard carton. An *ersatz Munitionkasten* ('substitute munition box'), developed to conserve scarce materials, was similar to the normal box but instead of a hinged lid, the projectiles were contained by four slats with gaps between them, nailed to the box's top.

Weighing 10.9kg and 1,651mm long, the RPzB 54 was about the same weight as an MG 34 machine gun but bulkier, as was the *Panzerschreck*'s ammunition. Man-packing the *Panzerschreck* was accomplished by slinging it muzzle-up behind the shoulder or slinging and carrying it horizontally at waist level. Another method was to simply rest it on the shoulder at a balance point to carry it at a comfortable angle. Carrying it vertically through forests with low limbs made the shoulder and waist positions more practical. If contact was not expected the launcher was unloaded and not cocked. If contact was expected the launcher was loaded, the weapon cocked, and the safety on – usually without the electrical contact plugged in. The shield was meant to remain attached. It could be detached when the weapon was transported in crowded vehicles or carried in the infantry cart.

Over longer distances, the principal means of transport for the *Panzerschreck* was the horse and a pair of the If 8 (Infanteriekarren 8, or 'infantry cart 8') carts assigned to each *Panzer-Zerstörer-Kompanie*. The If 8, a small, two-wheeled steel cart, weighed 81.5kg and could carry 350kg in the 1,190×990mm cargo compartment. It might have wooden-spoked wheels, steel disc wheels with steel or rubber tyres, or steel-spoked wheels with solid rubber tyres, all with shock absorbers. The two-shaft tongue fitted for the light draft horse could be replaced by a T-bar

**ABOVE** April 1945: armed with a Mk III Sten gun, this British soldier is taking prisoner two bicycle-mounted members of a German rearguard. It was common for two *Panzerfäuste* to be carried attached to a Truppenfahrrad 38 ('troop bicycle 38'), with the muzzle ends at the handlebars and the breech ends attached to the front-wheel fork. The Tommy has slung a captured StG 44 assault rifle on his shoulder. (© IWM BU 3197)

**ABOVE** Elements of 3. Panzer-Division serving in Italy and France, as well as other units, obtained several examples of the British Mk II Universal Carrier (AKA Bren gun carrier), what they called the Panzerjäger Bren 731(e). Assigned to *Panzergrenadier* units, these were given camouflage colour schemes and German markings. They were fitted with centreline racks for three *Panzerschrecke*, mounting brackets for four *Panzerfäuste* vertically (similar racks were fitted in the German *Kübelwagen* in reconnaissance units), and racks for 12 boxes of rockets on the rear. The *Panzerschrecke* were not fired from the Panzerjäger Bren; there was no elevating or traversing mechanism and attempting to aim them by finely orienting the tracked vehicle would be impossible. Instead, the vehicle served only to transport the *Panzerschrecke*; they were dismounted to fire. Note the leftmost *Panzerfaust* has a field-grey body while the nose cap and barrel are dark yellow, a common but non-standard colour scheme. (US Army)

**ABOVE** Members of a 14-man *Panzer-Zerstörer-Grupp* unload their six *Panzerschrecke* from the squad's two horse-drawn If 8 infantry carts. Typically, the lead cart was fitted with a unit-fabricated wooden-framed affair with four angled arms with notches and metal brackets allowing six *Panzerschrecke* to be carried. Nine ammunition boxes, stowed on their ends, could be carried in this first cart. The second cart could carry 12 more ammunition boxes, but usually fewer, along with *Panzerfäuste*, other anti-tank weaponry, smoke pots, etc. (US Army)

The *Panzerschreck* was viewed as more of a defensive weapon, so ammunition carriage was not a major concern. The gunner sometimes carried a rocket in one hand or a rocket in the tube. The loader might carry two rounds, either packed in the box transported by its rope handle or with one rocket in each hand. When moving short distances it was possible to carry two boxes totalling 22kg.

tongue, allowing the cart to be drawn by two men. Alternatively, the If 8 could be towed by a combination motorcycle or *Kettenkrad* half-tracked motorcycle. When the two carts were towed in tandem, the second cart had a short draw bar that hitched to the lead cart. The platoon headquarters had another pair of carts for reserve ammunition and individual packs. Basic load was ten rockets per *Panzerschreck*.

For the *Panzerschreck*'s ammunition the 698×228×172mm *Raket Munitionkasten* ('rocket ammunition box'), similar in construction to the *Panzerfaust*'s, was employed. It was smaller, holding only two 8.8cm rockets stowed pointing in opposite directions and held securely by three spacers on the bottom and two on the lid. A paper-wrapped replacement window piece (*Ersatzglas*) was in each box. There was a rope handle between the lid latches on the front. Boxes could be dark yellow, dark green, light grey, charcoal black or unpainted. 'R MUN' followed by the four-digit model number – '4322', for example – was marked on the lid in black. To the right was a symbol indicating the type of seasonal rocket motor: a circle indicated Wintermunition 1943/44, a cross meant Sommermunition 1944, and 'Arkt 44/45' meant Wintermunition 1944/45. 'BI' indicated *Blind*, an inert practice warhead with a live rocket motor. The temperature range for the specific type of rocket motors was printed on a paper label, for example 'Nur verschießen bei Außentemperaturen von -40°C bis +30°C' (Only for firing at outside temperatures of -40°C to +30°C). Also marked on the lid in smaller lettering was, for example, 'Heeres-munition Gesamtgewicht 11 kg' (Army ammunition, 11kg).

**ABOVE** The unit-fabricated *Aufsetzgestell für Munition* ('carrier frame for ammunition') held five 8.8cm *Panzerschreck* rockets. They were held in place by holes bored through the upper shelf and by metal bracket clips. The web and leather shoulder straps were from the Rückentrage 42 ('backpack frame 42'). Usually painted field grey (dark green), they may have been painted in any available colour. Being locally fabricated, there were variations in design. The *Panzer-Zerstörer-Kompanie* was authorized 34, but they were not always available. (US Army)

200mm of armour if striking at or near zero degrees. The size of the penetrating hole varied depending on the armour's thickness and the angle of impact. The entry hole was typically 25–38mm in diameter and the exit hole could be as small as 13mm wide. The blast overpressure inside an AFV or structure penetrated by a *Panzerfaust* was considerable. There was significant blast on the outside of the vehicle, but fragmentation from the thin sheet-steel body was minor, as it broke into a few large pieces. It could be devastating to infantrymen riding on – or on foot near – the target tank, however.

Owing to the large explosive charge, it was relatively effective against concrete, masonry, log and sandbag structures. Penetration effects are not reported, but are likely to have been at least twice as much as with armour.

## OPERATING THE *PANZERSCHRECK*

No fewer than eight manuals were published regarding the *Panzerschreck*. The first, dated 30 September 1943, was called *Panzerbeschußtafel 8,8cm R PzB 54*; it showed the vulnerable points of US, UK and Soviet tanks and was issued before the weapon was fielded. On 4 November 1943 a complete operator's instruction manual followed: *8,8cm R-Panzerbüchse*

American soldiers examine a *Panzerschreck* and its rockets. Many troops landing in Normandy were not yet aware of the *Panzerschreck* as it had been little encountered by US troops. It was not until after the Normandy battles that it began to appear in large numbers. This one has a fragmentation hole in the barrel over the punch generator. It is bent outwards, indicating that it penetrated from the other side. (Tom Laemlein/Armor Plate Press)

*54 (Ofenrohr) Richtlinien für Ausbildung und Einsatz.* A more detailed technical manual, *8,8cm R Pz B 54 mit 8,8cm R Pz B Gr 4322 Gebrauchsanleitung*, appeared on 6 January 1944, while *8,8cm R Pz B 54 mit 8,8cm R Pz B Gr 4322 – Schutzschild, Schutzbügel, verstellbares Korn mit Abdeckblech*, dated 24 February 1944, covered the added shield, improved sights and other upgrades. On 7 June 1944 *8,8cm R Pz B 54 mit 8,8cm R Pz B Gr 4322 Gebrauchsanleitung* replaced the January 1944 edition. A card showing vulnerable points on enemy tanks and named *Panzerbeschuß-tafel 8,8cm R Pz B 54 (Panzerschreck) mit 8,8cm R Pz B Gr 4322* appeared on 1 July 1944; 14 September saw the issue of a much revised operator's manual, *Panzernahkampfwaffen, Teil 1: Panzerschreck*, followed by a further revision including new ammunition information, *Panzerschreck 8,8cm R PzB 54 und R PzB 54/1 mit 8,8cm R PzB Gr. 4322 und 8,8cm R PzB Gr. 4992*, issued from 1 December 1944.

A Finnish soldier loads a *Panzerschreck*. The wooden connector holder can be seen still taped to the fin assembly. The contact pin that will be plugged into the black connector box can be seen on the top left side of the holder. The knife is a traditional Finnish hunter's knife – *puukko* – carried by many soldiers. (Tom Laemlein/Armor Plate Press)

## Selecting a firing position

The *Panzerschreck* could be fired from a kneeling or prone position. The standing position was not recommended as it was difficult to keep the launcher steady, unless the gunner leaned against a supporting tree or wall, for example. The weapon could only be fired from the right shoulder owing to the sights being on the left side. From the prone position or when firing from a slit trench, the launcher's hand guard was rested on the ground for stability. The shield was designed not to extend below the hand guard for this reason. In the prone position, both crewmen's legs had to be angled left away from the back blast area. The loader was also positioned on the left side, behind the gunner. He had to keep clear of the breech and ensure the back-blast area was clear of personnel, obstructions and flammable materials for at least 9m. Upon firing, the warhead was not armed for 3m; this allowed it to be fired through light vegetation and windowpanes.

## Preparing to fire

The first step in firing a *Panzerschreck* was to inspect the bore to ensure there were no obstructions. If there were small fragmentation holes in the tube, the weapon could still be fired so long as they did not obstruct the rocket and were located away from any part of the gunner's body. The front sight was adjusted for the estimated range and temperature variance. This was accomplished by setting it on the upper mark for winter ammunition and the lower for summer.

The gunner shouldered the weapon on his right shoulder, gripping the hand guard's forward grip with the left hand and placing his right hand on the rear grip with two fingers over the trigger. The cocking handle was pulled to the rear and the safety release caught to hold the handle to the rear. This action cocked the punch rod forward so it was not in contact with the punch generator. If the trigger was pulled at this point, it would not fire as the safety release was engaged.

## Loading the rocket

The loader loaded the rocket after checking to ensure it was clean and undamaged. If there was minor damage to the fin assembly and it could still be loaded, it was only to be used for firing practice as its accuracy was affected. He would also ensure the nose fuse's arming pin was still inserted and that its lead seal was unbroken. If the pin was missing or the seal broken, the rocket was not to be used.

The rocket was readied by pulling the retaining tape loose from the wooden handle with the contact plug and the firing wire pulled out of the fin assembly. The nose fuse arming pin was pulled and retained by the loader, who shouted, '*Vorstecker raus!*' ('Pin removed!'). At this point it was important that the rocket not be dropped, jarred or knocked against anything. If the pin was removed and there was no jarring, it could be reinserted and used later.

The rocket was loaded into the breech, ensuring the warhead's stepped shape did not hang on the breech's rim. The loader shouted, '*Granate ins Rohr!*' ('Projectile into tube!'). It was pushed in with the loader pressing down on the retaining latch until the leading edge of the drum stabilizer caught on the stop pin, which was forward of the contact pin. Caution was required to avoid pushing the rocket in too far. The drum stabilizer had to be in contact with the contact pin to be fired. The rear end of the fin assembly was flush with the breech rim. The latch served to prevent the rocket from slipping out. It had to be depressed to remove a rocket if not fired or it was a misfire. The loader inserted the plug into the connector box.

Here a Finnish soldier has pulled off the tape holding the wooden contact holder in place. The tape might be retained to tape the edges of the replacement glass issued in the rocket box for the blast shield's sighting port. The tape helped prevent the glass from cracking. It is obvious that the fin assembly is painted black and the rest of the rocket is field grey (dark green). He sits on a rocket ammunition box. (Tom Laemlein/Armor Plate Press)

## Firing the *Panzerschreck*

When ready to fire, the gunner depressed the safety release on the cocking handle and it sprang forward. The trigger was now engaged. The front and rear sights were aligned on the target's centre of mass or a specific vulnerable point if close enough. On the second- and third-model rear sights, lead marks were provided for taking flank shots at moving tanks.

The trigger was firmly pressed, ensuring the weapon was not jerked off-target. The punch rod snapped to the rear, striking the steel 'button' atop the punch generator with a sharp clack. The rod's shock travelled into the generator's moveable iron core, inducing an electrical current via a circular magnet and copper wire spool. A spring in the generator returned the core to its forward position. The electrical impulse travelled up the electrical wire from the generator to the connector box, into the contact plug, and into the rocket motor electrical igniter to ignite the motor. The Bakelite igniter housing was blown out of the tail up to 30m.

## Hitting the target

When the weapon was fired, there was a jet blast up to 3m to the rear with a great deal of smoke and dust. The rocket continued to burn for 2m beyond the muzzle, causing more smoke. Even in a light breeze this cloud dispersed quickly. The smoke could prevent the gunner from immediately seeing if he had scored a hit or missed and adjusting for a second shot if a miss. As the rocket motor was still burning when the rocket left the barrel, the protective shield 'caught' some of the propellant blast and caused a sight kickback. This was not severe, but the gunner had to be prepared for it. Unless in a dug-in position, the crew usually moved to another position before firing again, unless the target was disabled or they had missed and decided an immediate follow-up shot would be beneficial.

Troops of a *Panzerjagdtruppe* (tank-hunter team) of Fallschirmjäger-Regiment 6 use a knocked-out M4 tank for cover in Normandy, 1944. They are armed with a *Panzerschreck* (only small numbers were then available), a Pzf 60, and MP 40 submachine guns. Tank-hunter teams were often armed with a high percentage of automatic weapons to provide covering fire and drive accompanying infantry away from tanks. Note the straw tied to the *Panzerschreck* barrel forward of the blast shield and to the shield itself. The *Panzerfaust*-armed man carries a non-German flare-pistol case. Besides being used for signalling, flare pistols were employed to mark targets and blind tank gunners and drivers. (Tom Laemlein/Armor Plate Press)

## TACTICAL EMPLOYMENT

While *Panzerfäuste* and *Panzerschrecke* were mainly viewed as defensive weapons, they could be used offensively, especially the highly mobile *Panzerfaust*. Owing to these weapons' short ranges, they were most effectively employed from concealed positions. Ideally, enemy tanks would be engaged from the flanks and rear, with German positions selected that facilitated such engagements. Concealment was essential and the most lethal engagements were, in effect, ambushes. If tanks were close enough to be within *Panzerfaust* range, for all practical purposes they had broken through.

*Panzerschreck* employment tactics were more sophisticated than for *Panzerfäuste*. At the least, a platoon would be attached to a grenadier (infantry) battalion, with a squad attached to each company. This was in theory. Because of weapon and manpower shortages, it would not necessarily be so evenly structured. Also, there was no specific requirement for *Panzerschrecke* to be parcelled out equally to each unit and subunit. They would be attached to units as dictated by the terrain and avenues of approach.

In the attack, *Panzerschrecke* usually followed to the rear and were brought forward to engage tanks, field fortifications and defended buildings. It was common for a few to accompany the forward security detachment leading the unit. Divisions may have allocated some of their *Panzerschrecke* to the divisional fusilier battalion (*Divisions-Füsilier-Bataillon*), essentially a reinforced infantry battalion serving as a reserve or exploitation force having replaced the reconnaissance battalion.

In the defence, *Panzerschrecke* operated in troops, with three weapons situated in mutually supporting positions. Ideally, the regiment had its two battalions in the line with two grenadier companies each on the line and a company each in reserve. Each grenadier company would have two platoons forward and one in support – usually protecting a flank or gap, but the support platoon might be in the front line itself, depending on the frontage assigned a battalion. The *Panzerschreck* troops would be deployed in an interlocking web of mutually supporting fires. Of course deployment would not be so uniform on rugged terrain and in dense vegetation. They would be concentrated to cover avenues of approach. In forested, hilly terrain as found in much of Europe, they could be positioned along roads in depth – that is, one position after the other covering the road. Often they were positioned not to fire down the road, but hidden to take flank and rear shots.

The *Panzer-Zerstörer-Trupp* dug three positions, two forward and one to the rear, with a maximum of 150m between them, laterally and front-to-rear. Given unobstructed fields of fire, the troop in theory covered a sector 300m wide and 450m deep. Tanks passing the positions to the flanks could be engaged by all three *Panzerschrecke* as well as by dug-in adjacent *Panzerschreck* crews. The distance between positions would be reduced in rugged terrain and dense

Wearing the one-piece insulated winter uniform with camouflage side out, an infantryman waits with a Pzf 30 (groß) in ambush for an Allied tank. *Panzerfäuste* had to be protected from climate extremes. They functioned poorly if at all in subfreezing conditions. The sight and firing mechanism would not operate if iced over. The *Panzerfaust* had to be kept in the shade, avoiding direct hot sunlight. The weapon was particularly susceptible to moisture, especially the black-powder propelling charge. Black powder can be dried, but since the propellant charge was in a wax-coated cardboard cylinder fixed inside the launched tube, it was extremely difficult to do so. Water in the firing mechanism could cause it to fail. It was recommended that in fighting positions, a niche be dug into the side and *Panzerfäuste* be stored inside their wooden boxes or laid on a shelter-quarter or other canvas and covered. (Tom Laemlein/Armor Plate Press)

vegetation. Slit trenches were kept as narrow as possible for protection from strafing aircraft and air-bursting artillery. If at all possible the spoil was hauled off. This made detecting the position difficult and allowed the *Panzerschreck* to be aimed in any direction – *Rundumwirkung* (circular action) – without restricting the muzzle and ensuring no obstruction of the back blast. A *Kriechgrabe* ('crawl trench'), connecting the *Panzerschrecknest* to other positions, might run out of the apex of the 'V'.

Tank-hunting at close ranges, especially since tanks seldom operated alone or without infantry, demanded dedication and determination, what the Germans called *Kampfgeist* ('battle spirit'). Tanks could fight back. The coaxial, bow and turret-top machine guns were deadly, although the former was slow to track running enemy foot-soldiers. Tanks would cover one another with machine guns – 'back-scratching'. Tank crews were typically armed with pistols, grenades and one or two submachine guns. Accompanying enemy infantry often followed well to the rear to avoid fire directed at tanks, but close enough to provide protective fires.

The Germans published manuals showing four-view illustrations of the most common Allied tanks and their most vulnerable points. Typically, these were: the hull sides; the hull rear; the turret rear (less so the turret sides); driver's compartment; and where the fuel tanks and engine were located. Firing into the treads and road wheels could provide a 'mobility kill'. Once an enemy vehicle had been rendered immobile, friendly forces could conduct close-in attacks in order to finish it off – or, in some instances, the immobilized vehicle was simply left.

Enemy tanks were universally accompanied by dismounted infantry. In the case of the Russians, *tankodesantniki* ('tank riders') might ride into battle, but quickly dismounted when fired on. The Germans strove to separate the enemy infantry from the tanks. This was accomplished by fire from artillery, mortars and machine guns, usually with fires commencing

*Panzerschreck* in cover. *Panzerschrecke* were not too useful in dense forests owing to their very restricted range and the danger of hitting trees. The Germans established defences well inside forests rather than on the outer edge where they could be targeted by artillery and attacked by tanks. However, outposts would be positioned on the wood line backed by a few anti-tank guns and *Panzerschrecke* to engage and disorganize the attacking force before they entered the forest. Given that the *Panzerschreck* was heavier and bulkier than the US bazooka, it was ill-suited to stalking tanks within towns and forests. The *Panzerfaust* was more effective in these settings. (Cody Images)

A *Panzerschreck* is positioned for quick use on an earthen street barricade. The *Panzerschreck*'s comparatively short range did not hamper it in street fighting. A common tactic was to position them on side streets to get a side shot on Allied tanks as they crossed the intersection or slowly exposed themselves as they turned onto the side street. (Tom Laemlein/Armor Plate Press)

as soon as the attacking formation was within practical range. This also caused enemy tank formations to become disorganized, as commanders had to 'button up', restricting their vision – and were further hampered by smoke and dust. Besides high explosives, artillery and mortars fired smoke to blind tankers further. Forcing tankers to button up was extremely beneficial to *Panzerfaust* gunners as their position – and any manoeuvring on foot on their part – would be difficult to detect. Tank drivers were also hampered, as they normally could only see straight ahead and little, if at all, to their flanks. Each driver relied on his tank commander to detect threats and direct him to manoeuvre out of danger areas. A wily tank commander – what the Germans called a *Panzerfuchs* ('tank fox') – was noticed, as such commanders seemed to sense threats and wisely manoeuvred out of danger by second nature.

In combat, individual tank-hunters would take whatever shots presented themselves. Ideally, though, several individuals would open fire on the same tank from different directions. There are a few reports of

### The *Panzerschreck* map symbol

As with other individual small arms, the Germans did not devise a tactical map symbol for the *Panzerfaust*. At first, there was no specified symbol for the *Panzerschreck* either, not even in the new May 1943 publication *Merktafel über abgeänderte taktische Zeichen* ('Notification on Modified Tactical Symbols'). A symbol was provided, though, in the August 1944 publication *Panzernahkampfwaffen, Teil 1: Panzerschreck* ('Armour Close-combat Weapons, Part 1: Panzerschreck'). Since it was designated the *Racketen-Panzerbüchse* ('rocket [anti-]armour gun'), it used the old symbol for the *schwer Panzerbüchse* ('heavy anti-tank rifle'), that is, an anti-tank rifle over 8mm in calibre. It was modified with an open bottom semi-circle with a short line projecting from it in the direction of fire. Additionally, a small inverted 'V', the same symbol used to identify a *Nebelwerfer*, was placed inside the semicircle, indicating a rocket weapon. To the left of the symbol appeared '8,8', denoting 8.8cm.

British soldiers show a display of German infantry anti-tank weapons: RPzB 54, Pzf 30 (klein) and Pzf 30 (groß), and two *Tellerminen* (TMi 43 and 42 – 'platter' anti-tank mines). Lying in the weeds are Stg 24 ('stick') and Eihgr 39 ('egg') hand grenades. Once tanks were disabled or halted by obstacles, tank-hunters might close in with magnetic hand charges, Molotov cocktails and cluster charges made up of grenades and demolition charges. *Tellerminen* and demolition charges could be thrown into tracks or onto the engine deck. *Panzerschreck* troops usually had *Panzerfäuste* on hand to finish off halted tanks at close range. (© IWM B 8540)

*Panzerfäuste* being barrage-fired at tanks. With a tank and infantry breakthrough, the situation became disorganized and it was difficult to co-ordinate barrage firing. When accomplished, though, it was effective and presented too many targets for tanks to engage effectively. It was cautioned that the *Panzerschreck* be used only against AFVs; it did not generate sufficient fragmentation to be effective against troops in the open, as the thin sheet-metal body only broke up into a few large pieces. Troops riding on or walking beside tanks would suffer casualties, however. Even so, there were reports of barrage *Panzerschreck* firings at high angles against massed Soviet infantry attacks. The weapon could also be used against concrete, masonry, sandbag and timber structures.

Tank-hunter teams armed with *Panzerfäuste* and *Panzerschrecke* relied on an array of other weapons and munitions for their anti-tank mission, as well as hand and rifle grenades to engage accompanying enemy infantry. When selecting their armament, soldiers would of course consider the

This *Panzerschreck* gunner wears three *Sonderabzeichen für das Niederkämpfen von Panzerkampfwagen durch Einzelkämpfer* ('Special Badges for the Close Combat of a Tank by Single Combat'), also called the *Panzervernichtungabzeichen* ('Armour Destruction Badge') or *Panzerknackerabzeichen* ('Armour Knocker Badge'). The loader rams in a rocket. (Tom Laemlein/Armor Plate Press)

Panzerfaust

optimal range of the weapons available. Blinding smoke pots – emitting strong, acrid smoke so thick that if drawn into a tank it might drive the crew out – smoke candles and smoke grenades served several purposes. Thrown into the path of tanks, they blinded them, forcing them to halt or move slower. In rough terrain they might even blunder into ditches, gullies, rubble or other entrapping obstacles. They were blinded as tank-hunters moved in close to finish the kill. Smoke candles might be employed ahead of advancing enemy tanks, so they ran into a wall of smoke. Smoke was also laid behind tanks, allowing tank-hunters to close in on the tank's most vulnerable quadrant. Smoke screens could also be laid further away, to conceal the movements of tank-hunters.

Of course, the *Panzer-Zerstörer-Truppen* did not fight tanks alone. They were dug in among grenadier companies which formed their own tank-hunter troops and contributed rifle, machine-gun and mortar fire against enemy infantry. At night, when enemy tanks were moving toward German positions, machine-gunners would sweep long bursts of fire across their front. Tracers ricocheted off any tanks and *Panzerschrecke* and *Panzerfäuste* within range opened fire.

There is little argument that tank-hunting with close-attack weapons was extraordinarily dangerous. Germany instituted the *Sonderabzeichen für das Niederkämpfen von Panzerkampfwagen durch Einzelkämpfer* ('Special Badge for the Close Combat of a Tank by Single Combat') on 9 March 1942, but eligibility was backdated to 22 June 1941, the day the Axis invasion of the Soviet Union commenced. It was also known as the

## Flying *Panzerfäuste*

In the final death throes of the Third Reich all manner of desperate, last-ditch measures were undertaken. Most had little real impact or were simply not worth the effort. One of these was the *Panzerbekämpfung* (anti-armour combat) aircraft, in which a light trainer was mated with *Panzerfäuste*. In early March 1945, 12 Bücker Bü 181 C-2 *Bestmann* single-engine, two-seat trainers (*Schulflugzeuge*) were modified as tank-hunters. The low-wing aircraft was nicknamed the *Bestmann* as the student pilot and instructor sat side-by-side. *3.Panzerjagdstaffel* (armour-hunter unit) was composed of aircrews from Flugschule A/B 23 ('Flying School A/B 23') under Oberleutnant Karl-Heinz Dragenscheck. The unit was part of Schlachtgeschwader 2 ('Attack Squadron 2') – normally equipped with the Junkers Ju 87 Stuka – at Kaufbeuren in southern Germany. It was planned to field 14 such units with 12 aircraft and 20 pilots each, made up of instructors and students, both pilots and observer–navigators.

The otherwise unarmed trainers were each fitted with four Pzf 100s, one on the top and a second on the underside of each wing, outside the propeller arc. They were fired by Bowden cables running from the cockpit to the *Panzerfaust* triggers. Prior to take-off, the sights were flipped up and the *Panzerfäuste* locked in the ready-to-fire position to arm the launchers. A simple wire crosshair sight was fitted in the cockpit.

The tactics called for the tank-hunters to fly dawn and dusk sorties at tree-top level to avoid Allied fighter patrols. Flying this low made it extremely difficult to locate targets in Germany's forested, rolling terrain. The tank-hunters flew at 150km/h; when targets were located, they circled and made an attack run. At a distance of 500m they would climb to an altitude of 20m–30m and make a shallow dive on the – hopefully unsuspecting – enemy tanks. At 100m they fired all four *Panzerfäuste* and banked sharply to avoid the detonations and .50-calibre machine-gun fire. It was found that the back-blast from the top-mounted *Panzerfäuste* could set fire to the plywood wings and fabric-covered ailerons, so they were removed. This, of course, halved the already slim chances of a hit.

Only a few missions were flown in the last half of April in southern Germany. Usually, half the unit – six aircraft – would sortie. As far as is known, no tanks were ever attacked. They did manage to shoot up some trucks, as well as blow up German aircraft abandoned on airfields. The unit surrendered to the Americans at Reit im Winkl on 9 May. Two pilots defected with a *Panzerfaust*-armed Bücker to Switzerland, and it ended up in Swiss service along with five other Bücker trainers. A restored *Panzerfaust*-armed Bücker Bü 181 – not actually fitted with *Panzerfäuste* during the war – is on display at the Deutsches Technikmuseum in Berlin.

**LEFT** One of the 12 Bücker Bü 181 C-2 *Bestmann* trainer aircraft fitted with four remotely fired Pzf 100s – one on top and one on the bottom of both wings – in March 1945. Owing to the fabric and wooden wings catching fire, most had the upper *Panzerfäuste* removed. They proved rather ineffective. (US Air Force)

*Panzervernichtungabzeichen* ('Armour Destruction Badge'). The badge measured 3×8.5cm with a silver-coloured backing, black upper and lower edge braid, and a gunmetal PzKpfw IV tank. When a fifth award was earned, a single gold badge replaced preceding badges. It had a gold-coloured backing, black edge braid, and a gold, silver, or gunmetal tank. The badges were worn 'stacked' on the right upper sleeve. A certificate accompanied the badge. Its criteria called for a soldier to knock out a tank using a hand or rifle grenade, satchel charge, magnetic hand charge, or similar hand-delivered weapons. The *Panzerfaust* and *Panzerschreck* were included from 18 December 1943, the same date the gold version was authorized. There is no agreed figure with respect to the number of awards

made; estimates range from 14,000 to 18,000 awards, with fewer than 500 in gold. Oberstleutnant Günter Viezenz of Grenadier-Regiment 7 received the highest number of awards – 21. Alongside the *Panzervernichtungabzeichen*, the *Eisernes Kreuz* ('Iron Cross') was frequently awarded for particularly valorous anti-tank actions. Participating in an especially intense action could also result in the award of the *Nahkampfspange* ('Close Combat Clasp').

# THE *PANZERFAUST* AND *PANZERSCHRECK* IN OTHER HANDS

Nazi Germany sold *Panzerfäuste* and *Panzerschrecke* to its allies, who lacked similar lightweight portable anti-tank weapons. In fact, all of these countries were seriously deficient in all categories of anti-tank weapons. All used obsolete or obsolescent weapons, ranging from anti-tank rifles to small-calibre anti-tank guns. They also used captured and impounded weapons as well as higher-quality arms purchased from Germany. These were few in number as Germany could not make up its own severe shortages.

*Panzerfäuste* were used by Bulgaria as the Панцерфауст, Hungary as the *páncélököl* and Italy as the *Pugno Corazzato* – all direct translations

of *Panzerfaust*. The Romanians called it *pumnul blindat*, or 'armour dagger'. These countries usually received the Pzf 30 and Pzf 60 in relatively small numbers. Romania also used the *Panzerschreck* in modest quantities; in Romanian service, it may have been called the *frica blindate* ('armoured fear'), but this is unconfirmed. After the surrender of Italy, the *Panzerschreck* was also used by the German-trained forces of the RSI (Repubblica Sociale Italiana, or 'Italian Social Republic') in northern Italy. The Hungarians fielded a domestically produced 6cm rocket launcher, the *Páncélrém* ('tank fear'), appearing to be a cross between the US 2.36in M1 bazooka and the *Panzerschreck*. They may have called the *Panzerschreck* the same name, as they used it too.

Finland received the Pzf 30 (klein) and Pzf 30 (groß) in April 1944. They were first called the *Käsipatruuna* ('fist cartridge') and from August 1944, the *Panssarinyrkki* ('Panzerfaust') *F1* and *F2*. Finland also purchased 1,854 *Panzerschrecke*, which they designated the *88mm:n raketinheitin mallia B54* ('88mm of the rocket launcher model B54'), while the troops called it the *panssarikauhu* ('armour terror'). They remained in use into the late 1950s when they were replaced by the 55mm m/55 recoilless rifle (*sinko*) (with an 88mm over-calibre warhead) and were sold in the early 1960s to International Armament Corporation in the United States for sale to collectors.

The *Panzerfaust* also armed Nazi Germany's enemies. The Russians made extensive use of *Panzerfäuste*, calling the weapon the *Faust*, *Faustnik* (pl. *Faustniki*) and *Faustpatrone* (fist cartridge). *Panzerschrecke* also saw some use by the Soviets. The Polish resistance obtained a handful of *Panzerfäuste* and *Panzerschrecke* for use during the 1944 Warsaw Uprising. One account tells of partisans finding a *Panzerschreck* with two rockets. Having no idea how to load or cock it, they fired both rounds, almost incinerating themselves with the unexpectedly long back blast. Forcing the Germans' heads down, they survived to escape into the sewers.

Troops of the German-allied Royal Hungarian Army march to the front armed with *Panzerschrecke,* which they called the *Páncélrém* (tank fear). These appear to have been partly whitewashed. Over the shoulder was a common carrying position to include when moving through vegetation. The man behind the near-most *Panzerschreck*-carrying soldier shoulders a Pzf 30. (Tom Laemlein/Armor Plate Press)

A Red Army Guards soldier carries a Pzf 60. So many *Panzerfäuste* were captured that they were as familiar to, and as widely used by, Soviet soldiers as their own weapons. A German Eihgr 39 'egg' hand grenade is attached to his belt. (From the fonds of the RGAKFD in Krasnogorsk via Stavka)

During the Rhine crossing in March 1945, Britain's 1 Commando Brigade used *Panzerfäuste* for anti-tank defence. Some US units habitually used captured *Panzerfäuste*, especially for attacking buildings and fortifications. Other units restricted their use, for safety reasons or to prevent drawing friendly fire. The 82nd Airborne Division is reported to have used *Panzerfäuste* and *Panzerschrecke* frequently, even bringing some captured in Italy with them to Britain. Its commander recommended they be copied by the United States. Some US units carried *Panzerfäuste* in vehicles for emergency use. At least one tanker routinely carried a few in the turret rack for reconnaissance by fire, i.e. firing into suspected enemy positions and buildings. One account from the war's closing months tells of three US soldiers using a *Panzerfaust* to stalk and 'kill' a Tiger tank. They were given a week's leave in Paris, and so other soldiers followed suit. There was one instance in which the use of a *Panzerfaust* resulted in the presentation of the Medal of Honor. In September 1944 in France, 2nd Lieutenant Daniel W. Lee of the 117th Cavalry Reconnaissance Squadron fought off a strong counter-attack. He led a small patrol into the German rear. Separated from his men and wounded, he killed five Germans and drove off mortar crews. Finding a *Panzerfaust*, Lee hit a German armoured car and forced it to withdraw before he crawled back to his own lines.

# IMPACT
## Technology and tactics

After the defeat of Nazi Germany, captured *Panzerschrecke* were destroyed by lying them perpendicular on street kerbs or across shallow trenches and a bulldozer driving down the row. They were then recycled for the steel. Although the *Panzerschreck* was respected by Allied tankers – mainly because of its use in large numbers – there was little novelty about the weapon; it experienced numerous flaws and was heavy and awkward to handle. *Panzerschrecke* saw no post-war use other than by Finland, which

Finnish troops advance past a catastrophically destroyed Soviet T-34 tank. Two men each carry a Pzf 30 (groß). They are also armed with 9mm Suomi m/31 SJR submachine guns with 70-round drum magazines. (Tom Laemlein/ Armor Plate Press)

retained some – mostly in storage – into the late 1950s. Besides improved US bazookas, which remained in use after the war, a number of countries fielded similar improved bazooka designs after the war. The *Panzerschreck* was comparatively crude in comparison.

At the war's end, thousands of remaining *Panzerfäuste* were similarly blown up or dumped into the depths of the Baltic. Most existing *Panzerfäuste* today are from sold-off Finnish stocks. None saw post-war service in other armies. Even so, the *Panzerfaust* had a much greater influence on post-war infantry anti-tank weapons than did the *Panzerschreck*. The idea of a low-cost, single-shot, throwaway weapon that gave any soldier the ability to knock out a tank was an appealing one.

## THE *PANZERFAUST*'S DESIGN INFLUENCE

### Japanese anti-tank weapons

Like Nazi Germany's European allies, Japan lacked effective anti-tank weapons during World War II, and turned to the Germans – and the Americans – for inspiration. It is believed that Japanese technicians were not able to examine US bazookas until some were evacuated by aircraft to Japan from Leyte in late 1944. (There were no opportunities to evacuate captured weapons from earlier campaigns as the besieged islands were completely cut off.) These examples from Leyte would have been the two-piece M9A1 rather than the earlier one-piece M1 or M1A1. Development of a weapon equivalent to the bazooka commenced immediately, with shaped-charge data being provided by Germany. The result was the 7cm Type 4 (1944) rocket anti-tank gun (*rota ho*). It was not as effective as the bazooka, being heavier and achieving less armour penetration. A total of 3,500 were made, and were intended to be issued for the final defence of the Home Islands. They never saw combat.

The Germans also provided the Japanese with plans for *Panzerfäuste*, but the Japanese took a different track. They designed a reloadable 4.5cm anti-tank weapon designated the Type 5 (1945). Its 45mm tube was muzzle

The Japanese 7cm (actually 74mm – 2.9in) Type 4 rocket anti-tank gun was influenced by the US 2.36in M9A1 bazooka, but it incorporated its own design innovations. It was 1.5m long and weighed 8kg. Rather than an electric firing system, it used a percussion system with a pistol grip housing the trigger and hammer to fire a primer in the side of the rocket motor to ignite it. It had a two-piece breakdown tube, a simple iron sight and a folding bipod. The complete rocket weighed 4.08kg, rather heavy. The shaped-charge warhead was far from efficient, penetrating only 80mm. It was spin- rather than fin-stabilized and used a point-detonating mortar fuse, both counter-effective for shaped-charge rounds. (Mike Lebens, The National Museum of the Pacific War)

loaded. This had a 70mm-diameter, 2.3kg cylindrical, flat-nosed warhead lacking stand-off and fins. It was 'stabilized' by its tailboom containing the propellant charge. It had only a 30m range to penetrate 100mm of armour. There was a pistol grip and trigger near the breech with an abnormally long cone-shaped vent; 1m long (exclusive of the breech cone, approximately 36cm long), this 6.4kg weapon rested on the shoulder. Several variants were tested, but none adopted.

The Japanese 4.5cm Type 5 anti-tank weapon launched a poorly designed flat-nosed 70mm shaped charge. While influenced by the *Panzerfaust*, it was very different in design; it was reloadable, and offered poor performance in range and penetration. (US Army)

## Post-war *Panzerfaust* copies

Post-war copies of the *Panzerfaust* were fielded by two countries. Sweden produced two, the Pansarskott ('armour shot') m/45 and m/46. Elements of the m/45 looked very like a Pzf 60, notably the sight and trigger, but the Swedish weapon had a slightly shorter tube fitted with a cone-shaped blast deflector. The m/46 had an improved sight and trigger and the warhead had a cone-shaped nose cap with a detonator spike for stand-off detonation of its improved shaped-charge cavity. The Swedish weapons were painted dark green with a yellow band around the warhead's rear portion. The tube was marked in red with ELDSTRÅLE ('jet flame') and an arrow pointing to the rear. They were replaced by the Pansarskott m/68 'Miniman', a 74mm full-calibre, single-shot, throwaway anti-tank rocket launcher influenced by the US M72 light anti-tank weapon (LAW).

Argentina possessed a vibrant arms industry after World War II and fielded a number of domestic designs alongside copied and improved foreign designs. The PAPI (*proyectil antitanque para infanteria*, or 'anti-tank projectile for infantry') was similar to the Pzf 30 (groß), but had a smaller warhead with a large rim and a very different shaped-charge design. The sight and firing mechanism were similar to those of the Pzf 30 and it had a leather carrying sling.

The Argentine-made post-World War II *proyectil antitanque para infanteria* (anti-tank projectile for infantry – PAPI) was based on the Pzf 30 (groß). It was actually a less capable weapon than the Pzf 30. (US Army)

## THE *PANZERFAUST'S* TACTICAL INFLUENCE

During the latter stages of World War II, even the potential threat of the *Panzerfaust* could influence enemy tactics. US armoured infantry, which fought alongside tanks, very seldom rode their half-tracks into action and only infrequently used them for long-range machine-gun support. They fought dismounted and left their lightly armoured half-tracks in the rear. One reason for this was that the half-tracks were so vulnerable to *Panzerfäuste* and *Panzerschrecke*. US tank destroyers were more vulnerable than M4 tanks as they had much thinner armour and lacked coaxial and bow machine guns for close-in defence. One small advantage for

tank destroyers was that they had open-topped turrets. If the tank destroyer was hit, the internal blast overpressure was reduced.

## Post-war single-shot anti-tank weapons

From the early 1960s numerous countries fielded single-shot, throwaway shoulder-fired rocket launchers, beginning with the US M72-series light anti-tank weapon (LAW). These weapons were profoundly influenced by the *Panzerfaust* concept. The benefits of a light, compact anti-tank weapon packaged, shipped and issued as a single round of ammunition were quickly realized; such a weapon was logistically convenient and allowed hurried infantrymen to bring them rapidly into action. Packaged with several to a crate, their shelf-life is years.

The US 66mm M72 LAW was used by many countries and others were developed by the Soviet Union, Czechoslovakia, Poland, Yugoslavia, China, Sweden and France, ranging from 58mm to 105mm. Such weapons enabled infantrymen not only to knock out enemy AFVs, but also to engage field fortifications and buildings, and have been used against soft-skin vehicles and snipers. In effect, they have replaced rifle grenades. They are issued out to infantrymen in the same manner as hand grenades, that is, as needed. This all depends on the tactical situation and the types of targets. Insurgents have found them useful in that they are easily concealed and easy for marginally trained gunners to operate. They generally weigh less than 6.8kg, typically have a maximum effective range of 200–250m, and armour penetration varies from 300mm to 600mm. Most have a launcher tube-calibre warhead rather than the over-calibre warhead characteristic of the *Panzerfaust*. The single-shot disposable anti-tank rocket launchers of today directly owe their concept – if not design – to the *Panzerfaust*.

## Post-war reloadable anti-tank weapons

The *Panzerfaust* concept – a disposable, one-shot, one-man anti-tank weapon – went on to influence the design and employment of post-war reloadable, light, crew-served anti-armour weapons. In the past many crew-served anti-armour weapons required a multi-man crew owing to the weight of the weapon and its ammunition and mount. The *Panzerfaust* inspired weapons developers with the idea that weapons could be simplified and lightened. They searched for new lighter materials, simplified and efficient methods of operation, improved but lower-cost sights, and more lethal warheads and efficient propellants. It was also realized that such weapons did not have to be limited solely to employing anti-armour warheads, but also more specialized munitions such as anti-personnel, incendiary and fortification-defeating rounds.

Among the first one-man, portable, reloadable anti-armour weapons were the Russian RPG-series weapons.[1] During World War II the Red Army captured and used large numbers of *Panzerfäuste*, as they had no

1   See Gordon L. Rottman, *The Rocket Propelled Grenade*, Oxford: Osprey Publishing (2010).

comparable man-portable anti-tank weapons, but the Soviets did not produce their own *Panzerfäuste* from reverse-engineered examples as often claimed. Those *Panzerfäuste* that saw combat during World War II were single-shot throwaway weapons with crude sights, simplified percussion powder-train firing mechanisms, and no pistol grips. Conversely, the Soviet RPG-1 and RPG-2 were reloadable, had improved sights, and employed a rifle-like trigger and percussion firing-pin system with a pistol grip. The RPG-2 did take some inspiration from the Pzf 250, though; this weapon was to be reloadable and had other features similar to the future RPG-2, including a trigger grip and an electrical firing system. It had a long pointed-nosed projectile similar to the Pzf 150 and was intended to replace the *Panzerschreck*. It was scheduled for introduction in September 1945 and was not even built in prototype form. Both the United States and the Soviet Union obtained plans for the Pzf 250.

A variety of similar weapons were fielded from the 1950s and well into the 1970s, all owing at least some design features to the *Panzerfäuste*. Examples include the Soviet RPG-16, Chinese Type 70-I, Czechoslovak P27 *Pancérovka*, Yugoslavian RB M57 and M80 and Finnish m/55, all with 44–58mm launcher tubes and over-calibre warheads, with the exception of the Type 70-I. While these and similar weapons typically have a two-man crew – gunner and loader – they can be carried and easily operated by a single man. Since such weapons can knock out most tanks found on the battlefield today – even if only by a side or rear shot – their compactness and foot mobility over rough terrain and rubble allow the gunner to stalk AFVs while remaining concealed and able to manoeuvre into favourable firing positions.

Even though wire-guided and infrared-guided anti-armour missiles have now largely replaced recoilless rifles and larger shoulder-fired weapons, these light compact weapons influenced by the *Panzerfaust* provide valuable secondary and back-up weapons and are especially useful to insurgents, guerrillas and other irregulars.

The 66mm M72 LAW was adopted in 1963, first seeing combat in Vietnam. While such weapons are last-resort measures for defence against tanks, they have other uses. The M72, for example, was employed against defended buildings, field fortifications, soft-skin vehicles, troops in the open (for which shaped charges are of limited effectiveness) and even as an anti-sniper weapon. Barrage-fired into dense vegetation concealing enemy troops, they proved to be an effective means of suppressive fire. (US Army)

# CONCLUSION

The *Panzerfaust* and *Panzerschreck* provided German infantrymen with relatively effective and portable anti-tank weapons. They were not 'game-changers', however, being hampered by their limitations: short range, marginal accuracy, limited armour penetration, revealing back blast and – in the case of the *Panzerschreck* – weight and bulk leading to awkward handling. They were principally defensive weapons, but they gave infantrymen something they desperately needed, the ability to kill tanks at close ranges.

While the two weapons had only a limited impact on weapons design, the *Panzerfaust* profoundly influenced post-war anti-tank tactics, and the weapon's name lives on today. When the West German Heer was established in 1955 it was armed with US weapons, including the 3.5in M20A1B1 bazooka as the platoon anti-tank weapon. A modern *Panzerfaust* was developed by Dynamit-Nobel AG in 1960 – the Panzerfaust DM2 Ausführung 1 Lanze ('Model 1 Lance'), AKA the PzF 44. This was a reloadable weapon using the counter-mass recoil system to make it recoilless and reduced the back blast signature. It had a 44mm-diameter tube fitted with an optical sight, forward handgrip, rear pistol grip with trigger and a shoulder support. It was muzzle-loaded first with a long propellant cartridge containing powdered lead as a counterweight. This was the same weight as the warhead and countered the recoil. The 67mm shaped-charge warhead was then muzzle-loaded. It was 880mm long and weighed 6.9kg. Its effective range was 400m and the weapon could penetrate 370mm of armour.

Considered obsolete by the mid-1980s, the PzF 44 was replaced by the PzF 3 in 1990. It, too, was developed by Dynamit-Nobel AG. The PzF 3 consisted of a firing unit with the optical sight, fore handgrip, rear handgrip with trigger and shoulder rest. The over-calibre projectile and propellant were pre-loaded in launcher tube – a single unit. The tube with the projectile was attached to the firing unit. When fired, the tube was discarded and the

weapon reloaded. It, too, used the counter-mass recoilless system. The standard anti-armour round was a 110mm. There were also 90mm and 125mm anti-armour rounds and a number of special-purpose rounds, such as high-explosive plastic, fragmentation, smoke and illumination. Effective range was 500m. The firing unit loaded with a 110mm round weighed 12.9kg. At the time of writing the PzF 3 is still in use by eight countries and has been employed in Afghanistan. Neither of these post-1945 weapons owes much, if anything, to the original *Panzerfaust* in design terms, but it is striking that the name endures.

# GLOSSARY

| | |
|---|---|
| **AFV** | armoured fighting vehicle |
| **AP** | armour-piercing |
| **AT** | anti-tank |
| *Büchse* | an old term for a rifle |
| **FP 42** | Faustpatrone 42, or 'fist (hand) cartridge 1942' |
| **FP 43** | Faustpatrone 43, or 'fist (hand) cartridge 1943' |
| **FPZ** | *Faustpatronezünder*, or 'fist cartridge primer' |
| **GG/P 40** | Gewehrgranate zur Panzerbekämpfung 40, or 'rifle grenade for anti-armour combat 1940' |
| **GPzgr** | *Gewehr Panzergranate*, or 'rifle anti-armour grenade' |
| **GrB 39** | Granatbüchse 39, or 'anti-armour grenade rifle 1939' |
| *Gretchen* | 'Little Margaret'; diminutive for Gretel; nickname for Pzf 30 (klein) |
| *Haft-Hohlladung* | magnetic hollow charge (hand-delivered) |
| **HASAG** | Hugo Schneider Aktiengesellschaft ('Hugo Schneider Stock Company') |
| **HE** | high-explosive |
| **HWA** | Heereswaffenamt ('Army Weapons Office') |
| **kleine Zündladung 34** | 'small booster charge 1934' |
| **m/sec** | metres per second |
| *Ofenrohr* | (pl. *Ofenrohren*) 'stovepipe'; nickname for *Panzerschreck* |
| **PaK** | *Panzer-Abwehr-Kanone*, or 'armour defence gun', e.g. anti-tank gun |
| **PaK Pzgr 40** | Panzer-Abwehr-Kanone Panzergranate 40, or 'armour defence gun [anti-]armour projectile 1940'; an improved tungsten-shot AP round |
| *Panzerfaust* | (pl. *Panzerfäuste*) 'anti-armour fist [hand]' |
| *Panzerschreck* | (pl. *Panzerschrecke*) 'armour terror' |
| **Panzerwurfgranate 41** | 'anti-armour thrown grenade 1941' |
| *Pentol* | pentolite (explosive) |
| *Püppchen* | 'Dolly'; nickname for R-Werfer 43 |
| **Pzf** | *Panzerfaust*, or 'armour fist'; the abbreviation *Pzf* was very little used in World War II, but is used here when referring to the Pzf 30, Pzf 60, Pzf 100 and Pzf 150 for brevity's sake. The numbers indicate each model's optimal range in metres |
| **R-Werfer 43** | Rakentenwerfer 43, or 'rocket projector 1943' |
| **rds/min** | rounds per minute |
| **RPzB** | *Raketenpanzerbüchse* (pl. *Raketenpanzerbüchsen*), or 'rocket [anti-]armour gun', AKA *Panzerschreck* |
| **RPzBGr** | *Racketenpanzerbüchse Granate*, or 'rocket [anti-]armour projectile' |
| **Treibpatrone 318** | propelling cartridge (7.9mm for GrB 39) |
| **WASAG** | Westfalische Anhaltische Sprengstoff Aktiengesellschaft ('Westfalian Anhalt Explosives Stock Company') |

# BIBLIOGRAPHY

Chamberlain, Peter & Gardner, Terry. *Anti-Tank Weapons.* New York, NY: Arco Publishing, 1974.

Fleischer, Wolfgang. *Panzerfaust and Other German Infantry Anti-tank Weapons.* Atglen, PA: Schiffer Publishing, 1994.

Gander, Terry J. *The Bazooka: Hand Held Hollow Charge Anti Tank Weapons.* London: Parkgate Books, 1998.

Gander, Terry J. *Field Rocket Equipment of the German Army 1939–1945.* London: Almark Publications, 1972.

Natzvaladze, Yury A. *The Trophies of the Red Army During the Great Patriotic War 1941–1945: Vol. 1. Anti-tank Weapons, Aircraft Machine Guns, Assault Rifles.* Scottsdale, AZ: Land O'Sun Printers, 1995.

*Volkssturmmänner* speak their oath to fight to the death for Greater Germany. It was not uncommon for some *Volkssturmmänner* to march into combat armed with a single *Panzerfaust* and no individual firearm. Note that none have a rifle sling over their shoulder except for the man carrying an RPzB 54. (Tom Laemlein/Armor Plate Press)

# INDEX

Figures in **bold** refer to illustrations.